How to Write a Great Research Paper

A Step-by-Step Handbook

Revised Edition

Middle Grades

by Leland Graham
and Isabelle McCoy

IncentivePublications

BY WORLD BOOK
a Scott Fetzer company

Acknowledgements

The authors would like to gratefully acknowledge
the assistance and suggestions of the following people:

Maya Abel,
Major E. Bell, Jr., Shaina Bhanwadia,
Susanne Boden, Ann Evett, Barbara Heller,
Diane Lapointe, Jonathan McCoy,
Courtney Reed, Eric Tebbel,
and Josh Traynelis.

Cover by Geoffrey Brittingham
Illustrated by Kris Sexton

Print Edition ISBN 978-1-62950-014-0
E-book Edition ISBN 978-1-62950-015-7 (PDF)

World Book, Inc.
233 North Michigan Avenue
Suite 2000
Chicago, Illinois, 60601 U.S.A.

For information about World Book and Incentive Publications products, call **1-800-967-5325**, or visit our websites at **www.worldbook.com** and **www.incentivepublications.com**.

Printed in the United States of America by Sheridan Books, Inc.
Chelsea, Michigan
1st Printing May 2014

Table of Contents

Dear Student,

So you need to write a research paper . . .

The research paper is likely to be one of the most intimidating assignments that you will ever encounter. It's long—typically 500 words or more—and requires research, and, therefore, does not spring primarily from your imagination. Writing the research paper is a test of your ability to search out, recognize, accumulate, organize, and interpret a set of facts on a given topic. One of the chief goals of the research paper is to teach you how to find needed information from various sources.

You may ask, "Why should I write a research paper? What will I gain from writing this paper?" The most important thing you will learn is how to do research. This skill will assist you now and will become easier with each future paper that you write. Some educators believe that the sign of a good education is not how much you know, but how effective you are at locating what you need to know. Obviously, knowing how to properly research a topic is an important skill.

The length of your research paper will determine how long it will take to write it. The amount of time and research you will need for writing a twelve-page paper will differ drastically from that needed for a five-page research paper.

The quantity of information available in this age of technology is remarkable. Unfortunately, not all of this information is accurate. It is important to be able to evaluate sources. You will have to decide where to look for information and what information is acceptable. Do not be tempted to accept whatever information you find. Learn ways to effectively evaluate information. This skill will assist you in writing future papers. Evaluating sources is discussed in the section titled **Locating Resources and Materials**.

Today, most research papers are created, researched, and published electronically. You may type your paper on a computer, using a word-processing program such as Microsoft Word or Corel WordPerfect. Often your research will lead you to a variety of databases, Web pages, and/or search engines. There are many advantages to creating your research paper electronically:

- Files can be created on your home or school computer and published electronically.

- Hyperlinks (i.e., a word or image that when clicked will take the reader to another website) can be added to allow your reader to access additional information.

- There is also the potential to use multimedia such as illustrations, video, or sound in a presentation.

How to Write a Great Research Paper was designed to walk you step-by-step through the process of writing a research paper. This handbook will make the task seem less intimidating. It will provide you with an understanding of the process of writing the research paper, beginning with the selection of a topic and ending with the final "polish." Written in friendly language, the text moves through each step in the process and uses actual student examples. Activities provide you with practice in completing each step.

Several Important Notes:

- With the extensive use of electronic resources and easy-to-use search engines, the temptation to use someone else's research as your own is ever present. You need to learn to write your own research paper. Don't copy someone else's. Using another person's writing as your own violates the academic code of conduct. Stealing another person's words and claiming them as your own is called **plagiarism**. You must give credit to others for the use of their words and ideas.

- When you purposely turn in someone else's paper as your own, it is plagiarism. It is also plagiarism when you copy material into your paper without using quotation marks or citations to give the author credit. There are many rules dealing with research and the use of proper citations, and it is extremely important that you become familiar with them. Plagiarism will be addressed further in the section titled **Writing the First Draft**.

- The style of writing used in this handbook is based on the *MLA* (Modern Language Association) *Style Manual*. It is important to note, however, that there are other styles that may be used. Follow your teacher's instructions. The style used in your paper should be consistent, easy to use, and easy for the reader to understand.

This handbook will assist in making the research paper assignment less complicated and more readily understood. Hopefully, the experience you will gain by writing a research paper and following it through to the end will give you a sense of accomplishment. Once you have completed and presented your paper, you will have acquired an understanding of both the topic and the research skills involved in producing a well-written paper.

Best wishes with your research!

A Great Research Paper

Evaluate.

Polish.

Prepare works cited list.

Write final draft.

Revise and rewrite first draft.

Write first draft.

Outline information.

Write thesis statement.

List points to make.

Take relevant notes.

Prepare works cited cards.

Locate resources and materials.

Choose topic.

Determine purpose of paper.

How to Write a Great Research Paper, Revised Edition

Selecting Your Topic and Getting Organized

What Is a Research Paper?

A research paper is an investigative, written report based upon information compiled from a variety of sources. Your school, your local library, and the Internet will contain most of the resources and materials you will need for the research paper. Such resources include websites, encyclopedias, dictionaries, periodicals, newspapers, and many other reference sources. Most teachers who assign research papers are concerned not only with the finished product, but also with the process involved in obtaining the information. This process will be introduced, practiced, and examined in this guide. Follow the handbook step-by-step through the process, and you will discover much more than you initially anticipated.

What Is Your Role as a Researcher?

To begin the process of research, you must identify your role as a researcher. You will need to investigate, examine, clarify, and defend your subject. You should supply graphs, charts, or diagrams if they are pertinent to your topic. The tone that you use in writing must be indicative of the research process. And, most importantly, be sure to give credit to sources that you use in your paper.

Create a Research Folder

Prior to beginning work on the paper, organize your materials in a folder. Many teachers require all working materials to be submitted at the end of the research process. Your folder will also serve as an easy reference for future assignments on this topic.

Think About It!

- Select a topic that you find interesting.

- Follow your teacher's guidelines carefully.

- Schedule your time wisely and work steadily every day.

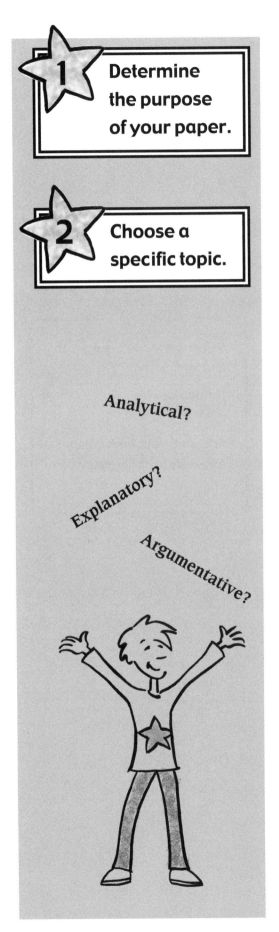

1 Determine the purpose of your paper.

2 Choose a specific topic.

Analytical?

Explanatory?

Argumentative?

What Is the Purpose of Your Paper?

In a research paper, your task may be:
- to explain,
- to analyze, or
- to argue.

In an **explanatory** paper, you will give factual information to your audience. You may define and describe a topic. For example, you may choose to define penny stocks and explain how they have made some individuals wealthy. Another explanatory paper might trace and describe the origin of Greek mythology.

When writing an **analytical** paper, you must thoroughly investigate a subject. You will examine the different elements of your topic and compare and contrast those elements. Researching the Creek Indians and their customs might require an analytical paper. As a researcher, you might analyze heart attacks and their causes, preventions, and treatments.

If you are writing an **argumentative** paper, you will choose a position on a topic and defend your position. If you are researching violence on television, you may choose to argue that violence causes aggressive behavior in teenagers. An argumentative research paper often answers a question posed by the topic, such as "Can we save the ozone layer from destruction?"

Choosing the Topic

When choosing a topic for a research paper, it is important to select one that is interesting to you—a subject about which you have always wanted to learn more or an adventure into an entirely new realm of study. Students sometimes are tempted to describe and narrate their personal experiences (for example, "A Week at The Beach" or "My Life as a Younger Sister or Brother") for their research paper. A research paper is an investigative report based on facts or theories, so a description of personal experiences alone is not appropriate. It is possible, however, to write a factual paper on a subject that genuinely interests you. For example, you may write your research paper on "Football and Personal Fitness."

In selecting a topic, your teacher may identify the broad (or general) subjects for your research paper. Then it will be up to you to find a specific (or narrower) topic to research. For example, if your teacher were to assign a research paper on the general subject of dinosaurs, your task would be to divide this general subject into specific, narrower topics. You might begin the task of identifying appropriate topics by asking such questions as these about the subject:

- How would you describe Earth's vegetation during the time of dinosaurs?
- How would you describe the climate during this era?
- How are dinosaurs classified in the animal kingdom?
- What are some physical characteristics of dinosaurs?

Problems to Avoid

Avoid these pitfalls when selecting your topic:

- Topics that are too limited
  Example: *What Is the Panama Canal?*
  Better Topic: *How Do these Famous Canals Compare: Panama, Suez, and Erie?*

- Topics that are too broad
  Example: *What Is Earth's Weather Like?*
  Better Topic: *Do the Moon's Phases Affect Earth's Weather?*

- Topics that have little or no available information
  Example: *Why Did Mary Queen of Scots Like to Play Golf?*
  Better Topic: *What Impact Did Mary Queen of Scots Have on Scotland?*

- Topics that are confusing because they do not make clear what information is to be addressed
  Example: *What Did Mark Twain Like?*
  Better Topic: *How Did Mark Twain's Interest in the Mississippi River Influence His Writings?*

- Topics that ask questions based solely on opinion
  Example: *What Is the Best Math Game?*
  Better Topic: *What Is Game Theory and Where Is It Applied?*

Think About It!

- Independently browse, brainstorm, question, predict, and focus as you consider the general subject.

- Before you make a final decision about your topic, check the library and the Internet to review the sources available on this topic.

- If your topic is relatively new or technical, you may have difficulty finding all of the information you need for your paper.

The most important step in writing a research paper is selecting an appropriate topic.

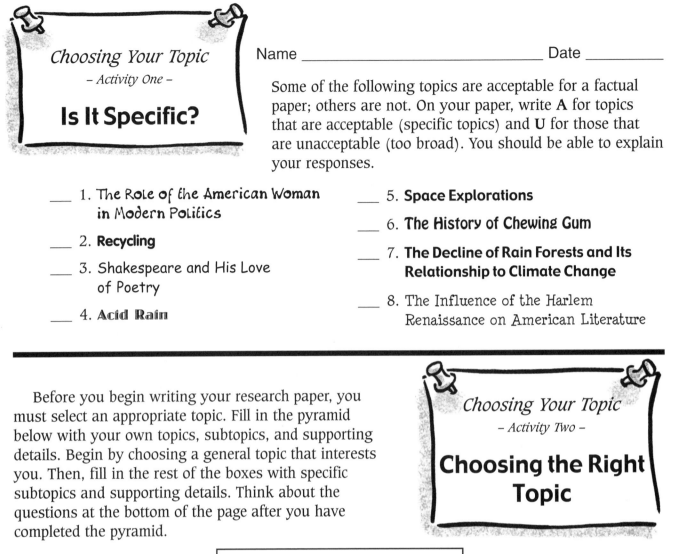

Choosing Your Topic
– Activity One –

Is It Specific?

Name _____ Date _____

Some of the following topics are acceptable for a factual paper; others are not. On your paper, write **A** for topics that are acceptable (specific topics) and **U** for those that are unacceptable (too broad). You should be able to explain your responses.

___ 1. The Role of the American Woman in Modern Politics

___ 2. **Recycling**

___ 3. Shakespeare and His Love of Poetry

___ 4. **Acid Rain**

___ 5. **Space Explorations**

___ 6. **The History of Chewing Gum**

___ 7. **The Decline of Rain Forests and Its Relationship to Climate Change**

___ 8. The Influence of the Harlem Renaissance on American Literature

---

Before you begin writing your research paper, you must select an appropriate topic. Fill in the pyramid below with your own topics, subtopics, and supporting details. Begin by choosing a general topic that interests you. Then, fill in the rest of the boxes with specific subtopics and supporting details. Think about the questions at the bottom of the page after you have completed the pyramid.

Choosing Your Topic
– Activity Two –

Choosing the Right Topic

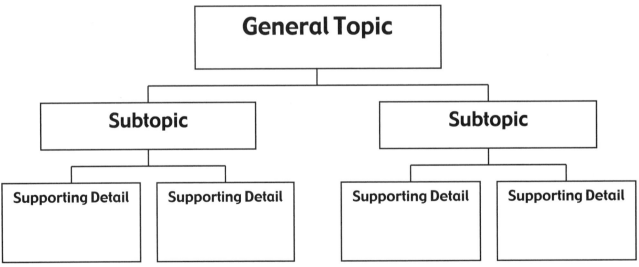

| General Topic |
| Subtopic | Subtopic |
| Supporting Detail | Supporting Detail | Supporting Detail | Supporting Detail |

1. How long is your paper supposed to be? *(Your topic should be limited enough to be covered thoroughly, but broad enough to be the subject of an interesting discussion.)*

2. Do you like your chosen subject? Which features of the general subject interest you most?

3. Is there enough available information?

Name _____ Date _____

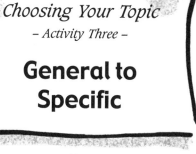

> **When you select your topic, begin with a general subject, such as** *Learning to Speak a Foreign Language.* **Then think of a specific topic, such as** *Learning to Speak Spanish.*

Look at the subjects below. Then write a topic for each subject that might be of interest to you if you were writing a research paper. Finally, circle the specific topic that would interest you the most.

GENERAL SUBJECTS	SPECIFIC TOPICS
Science Experiments	_____
Native Americans	_____
Music	_____
Natural Disasters	_____
American Authors	_____
Space Explorations	_____
Technology	_____

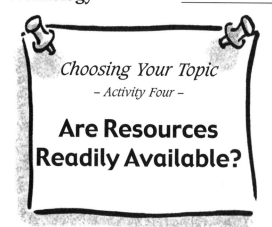

Using the topic you circled in Activity Three, locate a variety of resources (newspapers, magazines, books, encyclopedias, dictionaries, almanacs, interviews, and online resources) that you could use to learn about the topic. List at least six actual resources.

TOPIC: _____

RESOURCES | PAGE(S) OR VOLUME OR WEB ADDRESS

1. _____ _____

2. _____ _____

3. _____ _____

4. _____ _____

5. _____ _____

6. _____ _____

Getting Organized

– Activity Five –

Planning Calendar

Name _____ Date _____

It is important that you plan your research paper properly. Use this monthly planner to record all the deadline dates for each step you will follow in writing your paper. Decide how much time each week you will need to allot to complete the steps.

Sunday	Monday	Tuesday	Wednesday	Thursday	Friday	Saturday

How to Write a Great Research Paper, Revised Edition

Name _____ Date _____

Staple this progress checklist inside the front cover of your research folder. Check off the steps in order as you write your research paper.

Steps	Date Assigned	Date Due	Completed
1. Determine the purpose of your paper.			
2. Choose your topic.			
3. Locate resources and materials.			
4. Prepare a works cited card for each of your sources.			
5. Take relevant notes.			
6. List the points you wish to make.			
7. Write a thesis statement.			
8. Outline the information you have gathered. (This is your preliminary outline.)			
9. Write your introduction.			
10. Write the body of your paper.			
11. Write the conclusion.			
12. Revise and rewrite your first draft.			
13. Write your final draft.			
14. Prepare your works cited list.			
15. Polish your paper.			
16. Evaluate your paper.			
17. Present your paper.			

Evaluate.

Polish.

Prepare works cited list.

Write final draft.

Revise and rewrite first draft.

Write first draft.

Outline information.

Write thesis statement.

List points to make.

Take relevant notes.

Prepare works cited cards.

Locate resources and materials.

Choose topic.

Determine purpose of paper.

Now you're ready to . . .

Locating Resources and Materials

Writing a research paper requires that you learn to find and use print and electronic resources and materials. The library reference section has a variety of places where you can begin your search. Dictionaries, almanacs, encyclopedias, and Internet search engines are just a few useful starting points. Sometimes library materials cannot be checked out, but most libraries will allow you to photocopy or print out information you may need.

Resources to Consult

- **The Librarian/Media Specialist**
  An important resource available to you is your school's librarian or media specialist. This person is a virtual "walking encyclopedia" of information just waiting to answer your questions and help you. In addition, the librarian knows the location of the resources in the library, understands how to use the computers, and can suggest other ways to find quick, reliable information. Do not hesitate to make use of this resource.

- **Encyclopedias**
  There are many kinds of encyclopedias, so take time to browse through and become acquainted with them. An encyclopedia offers a variety of articles (usually brief) on many different subjects. Often encyclopedias can be found online. Using an online encyclopedia allows you to search easily for a particular topic.

  When starting your research, it is a good idea to check the encyclopedia first for a "bird's-eye view" of your subject before moving on to more detailed sources. For example, if you are doing a research paper on how Mark Twain's life influenced the subject matter in *The Adventures of Tom Sawyer*, you might look up "Twain" in the encyclopedia to get an overview before checking the other materials.

- **Dictionaries**
  Use the standard dictionary as an easy reference to spelling, syllabication, word origin, and parts of speech, as well as definitions. Don't ignore biographical dictionaries, such as *Chambers Biographical Dictionary*, which supply information about famous people's lives.

3 Locate resources and materials.

Think About It!

Don't forget to use your own experience!

One of the most important resources is YOU! You can use your own personal experiences in writing your paper, regardless of the research topic.

- **Atlases**

  If you are a student who enjoys learning about different cities and countries of the world, then you will want to learn to use the atlas. There are many types of atlases, but they all share some similarities. An atlas is a book of maps and much more. An atlas contains information and facts about climate, industries, natural wonders, resources, population, history, imports, and exports. For example, you may find in the atlas the location of Cairo, Egypt, information on its climate, population statistics, and the name of Egyptian landmarks and monuments. Some important atlases with which you should become acquainted are the *National Geographic Atlas of the World*, *The Times Comprehensive Atlas of the World*, and the World Book *Atlas of the World*.

- **Almanacs**

  Almanacs are a unique source of facts and information. An almanac can help you find which phase of the moon would be appropriate for planting a short row of English peas. You can find a list of the all-star baseball games or a list of actors and actresses who won Academy Awards in 1974. Almanacs, which are published annually, are ideal sources for up-to-date, miscellaneous information on current events. Common almanacs that you may find in your library include the *TIME Almanac* and *The World Almanac and Book of Facts*.

- **Audio and Video Resources**

  Have you thought about using CDs, videos, and DVDs as references in your research paper? There are many situations in which this is a good idea. For example, if you are researching music of the 1960s, you may listen to recordings by the Beatles, the Doors, Elvis Presley, and Diana Ross and the Supremes.

• Other Resource Materials

The library has many more references with which you will become familiar. Here are just a few examples of valuable resources you can find in your library. Many of these resources are available online.

American Men and Women of Science
Bartlett's Familiar Quotations
Benet's Readers' Encyclopedia
The Cambridge Encyclopedia of the English Language
Contemporary Authors
CultureGrams
Current Biography
Dictionary of American History
Dictionary of Scientific Biography
DK Children's Illustrated Encyclopedia
Encyclopedia of African History and Culture
Encyclopedia of Religion
Encyclopedia of World Biography
The Grove Dictionary of Art
Grzimek's Animal Life Encyclopedia
Handbook of North American Indians
International Encyclopedia of the Social Sciences
McGraw-Hill Encyclopedia of Science and Technology
The New Grove Dictionary of Music and Musicians
Occupational Handbook
Oxford Companion to American Literature
Oxford Companion to English Literature
Oxford Encyclopedia of Theatre and Performance
Oxford English Dictionary
Oxford Dictionary of Quotations
Play Index
Short Story Index
The Timetables of History
Today's Science
Twentieth Century Authors
Van Nostrand's Scientific Encyclopedia
World Authors
The World Book Encyclopedia
The World Factbook

If your library does not have a certain book or article you need, your librarian may be able to order the materials through the inter-library loan system.

Choosing Resources

– Activity One –

Using Available Materials

Name _____ Date _____

Answer the following questions. Refer to an atlas, encyclopedia, dictionary, almanac, and other resources as needed.

1. Who is the head librarian/media specialist of your school? _____

2. Where will you look for an article on Michael Jordan's retirement speech from basketball?

_____

3. What was the population of Atlanta, Georgia, in 2010?

_____

4. Name two novels written by E. B. White.

    a. _____

    b. _____

5. What source provides an explanation for the disappearance of dinosaurs?

_____

6. List the birth dates and birthplaces of the following people.

    a. Marc Anthony _____   _____

    b. Bill Cosby _____   _____

    c. Steven Spielberg _____   _____

    d. Bill Clinton _____   _____

7. Find a magazine article written about each of the following subjects.

    a. Native Americans   _____

    b. King Tutankhamen   _____

    c. Walt Disney World _____

8. Answer the following about your home state.

    a. Capital city   _____

    b. Population   _____

    c. Biggest tourist attraction   _____

How to Write a Great Research Paper, Revised Edition

Computers and the Library

Computers in libraries have made books, periodicals, and other materials much more accessible to students. A computer can search for materials on any subject and display the information on the screen. It can tell you exactly where to find a specific book on the library shelves. By using the Internet, you can promptly retrieve research on any topic. You can also use a computer to access online databases.

Computers also make it easier to write your research paper. You can make changes or edit your draft instantly, and you can quickly "spell check" your work. The electronic thesaurus on your computer can be used to avoid repeating the same word too many times. If you have difficulty with a computer, do not hesitate to ask the librarian for help.

This section discusses some specific computer uses:

Online Catalog

In the majority of libraries, the online catalog has replaced the manual card catalog. There are three ways that you can search for information using the computerized catalog:
- by subject
- by title
- by author

With the online catalog, you can quickly acquire a print-out for books on any given subject, as well as information on the current availability of the books in the library. The list will contain books on your topic identifying the title, author, and call number. Since books are placed on the library shelves in alphanumeric order, the call number is extremely important!

Books are listed by title, by last name of the author, and by subject. In order to locate information about your topic, use the computer to conduct a search using key words, such as "Hurricane Katrina" or "Spanish." Once you have entered your key word(s), the computer will list a number of sources on your topics.

What's a call number?

A CALL NUMBER is an alphanumeric code given to each book in a library. This code tells people where to find books about specific topics.

Look it up!

By Subject

Look it up!

By Title

Look it up!

By Author

The Internet is a great telecommunication system when used properly! Instead of searching for a word in a book, you can use a search engine to locate a list of websites on your topic.

The Internet

The Internet is an extremely popular reference tool in schools and libraries, and all over the world. The Internet can be used to explore a topic in a manner similar to searching in an encyclopedia. Information found on the Internet is obtained from places outside your school and even outside your own country. Some search engines that are commonly used include Bing, Google, and Yahoo!

If you are writing a paper on the history of the Hawaiian Islands before they became part of the United States, you can search the Internet to obtain the needed information. Just search using the key words "History of Hawaii" or "Hawaii before statehood." Not only is text available, but sound and video images will provide valuable information. The Internet allows you to interact daily with a huge amount of information that circles the globe at the speed of light.

With online databases, you can enter search terms and get a variety of results on your topic. In addition, your search can be expanded. For instance, an article about astronaut Neil Armstrong might also have links to articles about the educational requirements for an astronaut, or what kind of training certain astronauts received.

One hint for using Internet search engines: If you wish to narrow your search, use quotation marks around your key words. Using quotation marks will indicate that all the words must appear together in the same order in which they were typed.

A Word of Warning

It is extremely important to evaluate your sources when using the Internet. Many websites contain accurate and useful information, but others are unreliable. Here are a few ways to determine the reliability of a website:

- Read the Web address or URL (Uniform Resource Locator). You can usually rely on Web addresses that end in ".gov" or ".edu."

- Learn about the author/publisher. Most reliable Web pages will provide the following information: the name and contact information of the page owner, the last date the page was updated, and a link for questions or comments.

- Ask your librarian, parent, or teacher if you are uncertain about the accuracy of a website.

Evaluate Online Resources

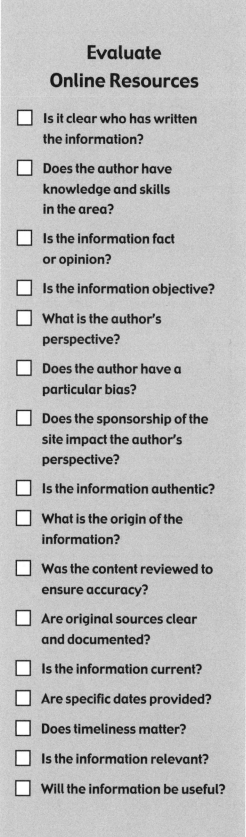

- ☐ Is it clear who has written the information?
- ☐ Does the author have knowledge and skills in the area?
- ☐ Is the information fact or opinion?
- ☐ Is the information objective?
- ☐ What is the author's perspective?
- ☐ Does the author have a particular bias?
- ☐ Does the sponsorship of the site impact the author's perspective?
- ☐ Is the information authentic?
- ☐ What is the origin of the information?
- ☐ Was the content reviewed to ensure accuracy?
- ☐ Are original sources clear and documented?
- ☐ Is the information current?
- ☐ Are specific dates provided?
- ☐ Does timeliness matter?
- ☐ Is the information relevant?
- ☐ Will the information be useful?

Setting Up An Interview

1. Contact the person to be interviewed and set up the interview.

2. Prepare a list of relevant questions.

3. Record the name and position of the person interviewed, the time, the place, and the date of the interview.

4. Dress appropriately and show up on time.

5. Conduct the interview in a professional manner.

6. Thank the expert.

Additional Resources

Interviews

To obtain information, you may need to talk with a person who is an expert on your topic. An interview may be conducted in person, over the telephone, or through the Internet (e-mail or online chat). In addition to receiving this expert's opinion, you may also receive first-person accounts or references to other places or people.

When setting up an interview, you will need to explain your purpose and your topic. Prepare a list of questions in advance. (Include both factual and open-ended questions.) Record or take notes so that you can remember the information accurately. If you wish to record the interview, be sure to ask permission. Document the subject, date, place, and time of the interview.

Newspaper Articles

Newspaper articles are a valuable resource for up-to-the-minute information on your topic. You can use the Internet to locate newspaper articles. Most major newspapers have their own websites. These websites usually offer an indexed list of articles that have been published. Follow the directions on the website to access the articles.

Television and Radio

Two other sources of up-to-date information are radio or television. Check your local television and radio program listings for information concerning your topic. Public Broadcasting Service (PBS) and National Public Radio (NPR) offer a wide variety of educational programs.

Surveys

Conduct a survey in your school or community on your topic. Begin by designing a questionnaire. The questions used should be clear and easy to understand. Questions that require a *yes* or *no* response are easy to tabulate. Questions that use a rating scale to evaluate people's opinions are also easily tabulated. Document the number of people surveyed, the date, and location of the survey.

Name _____ Date _____

Using the computers available in your library,
complete the following tasks.

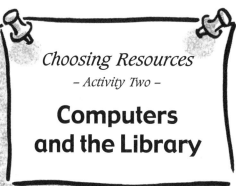

1. Look up the Royal Canadian Mounted Police in an online
   encyclopedia and summarize an important fact from the entry.

   _____

   _____

2. Look up the Bermuda Triangle and list the names and call numbers of at least two pertinent
   books available in your school library or media center.

   a. _____

   b. _____

3. Find a book, encyclopedia, newspaper, or magazine article on John F. Kennedy. Document the
   source below.

   _____

   _____

4. Locate and document a source on American music and culture of the 2000s.

   _____

   _____

5. Locate and document a source on Martin Luther King, Jr. and the Civil Rights Movement.

   _____

   _____

6. Locate and document two sources on Native American tribes that occupied the Oklahoma
   Territory.

   a. _____

   b. _____

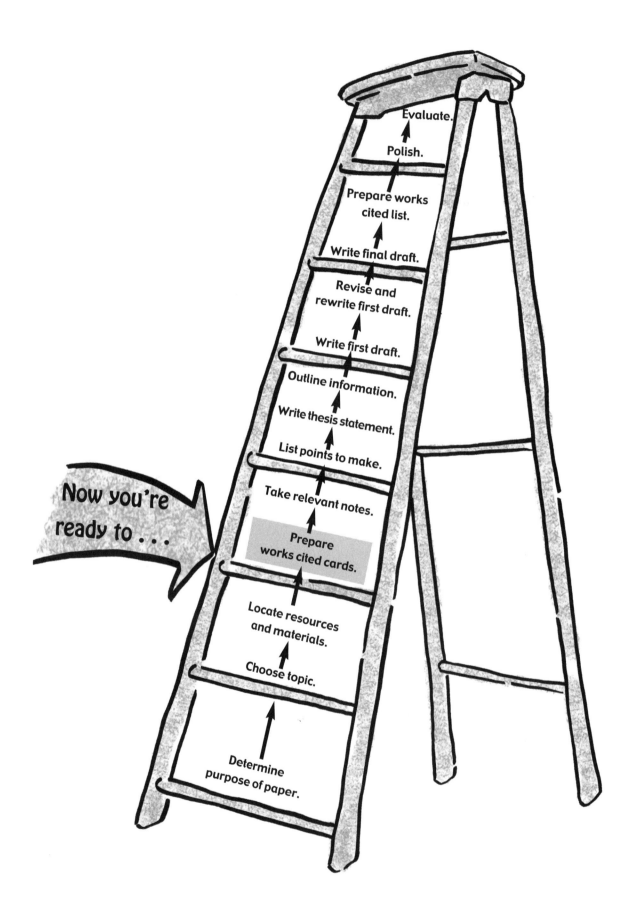

Evaluate.

Polish.

Prepare works cited list.

Write final draft.

Revise and rewrite first draft.

Write first draft.

Outline information.

Write thesis statement.

List points to make.

Take relevant notes.

Prepare works cited cards.

Now you're ready to . . .

Locate resources and materials.

Choose topic.

Determine purpose of paper.

Writing
Works Cited Cards

Any time you find an information resource that you want to use in your paper, you should document it by making a works cited card. Record the required source information on index cards or papers cut to a standard size. Using card-sized notes will make alphabetizing the resources easier and allows you to add or delete references without having to recopy an ordered list. Number the cards. The numbers will come in handy as you begin to take notes.

These cards will be an important resource as you eventually create your works cited list. Each type of resource will require you to record different information on the card. Check the guidelines below to make sure you record the information you will need when you prepare your final list. The examples shown in this section are based on the MLA style guidelines.

Documenting Print Sources

For a book with one author:

- Author's last name, author's first name
- Title of the book (underlined or in italics)
- Edition (if other than first edition)
- Place of publication
- Name of publisher
- Year of publication (most recent)
- Medium of publication (Print)

> ⑤
>
> Kuoche, Lawrence David. _The Bermuda Triangle Mystery-Solved._ New York: Harper and Row, 1975. Print.

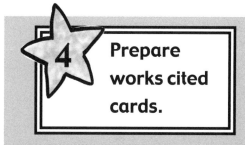

4 Prepare works cited cards.

Punctuation Pointers

A comma is placed between the author's last and first names.

A period is placed after the author's name and the book title. The book's title should be underlined (if writing by hand) or in italics (if typing on a computer).

A colon is placed after the name of the city.

A comma is inserted between the name of the publisher and the year of publication.

A period is placed after the year and the medium of publication.

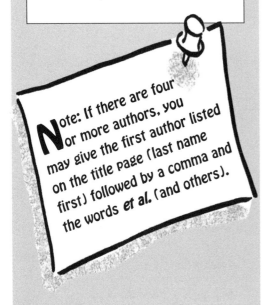

Note: If there are four or more authors, you may give the first author listed on the title page (last name first) followed by a comma and the words *et al.* (and others).

For a book with multiple authors:

- Authors' names—the name of the first author listed on the title page (last name first), followed by other authors
- Title of the book (underlined or in italics)
- Edition (if other than first edition)
- Volume (if a multivolume work)
- Place of publication
- Name of the publisher
- Year of publication (most recent year)
- Medium of publication (Print)

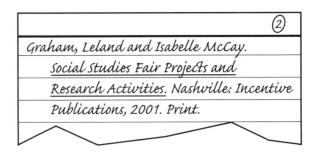

Graham, Leland and Isabelle McCay. *Social Studies Fair Projects and Research Activities.* Nashville: Incentive Publications, 2001. Print.

For an encyclopedia article with an author:

- Name of the author of the article
- Title of the article (in quotation marks)
- Title of the encyclopedia (underlined or in italics)
- Year of publication (edition)
- Medium of publication (Print)

Griffiths, Ralph A. "Richard III." *The World Book Encyclopedia.* 2013 ed. Print.

For an encyclopedia article with no author listed:

- Title of the article (in quotation marks)
- Title of the encyclopedia (underlined or in italics)
- Year of publication (edition)
- Medium of publication (Print)

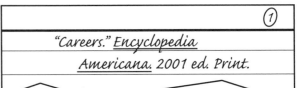

"Careers." *Encyclopedia Americana.* 2001 ed. Print.

For a magazine or newspaper article with an author:

- Name of the author
- Title of the article (in quotation marks)
- Name of magazine or newspaper (underlined or in italics)
- Date of magazine or newspaper (day, month, and year)
- Newspaper section letter or number (if not part of page number)
- Page number(s)
- Medium of publication (Print)

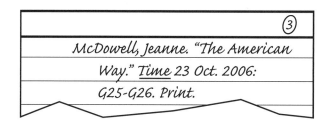

③

McDowell, Jeanne. "The American Way." _Time_ 23 Oct. 2006: G25-G26. Print.

For a magazine or newspaper article with no author listed:

- Title of the article (in quotation marks)
- Name of magazine or newspaper (underlined or in italics)
- Date of magazine or newspaper
- Newspaper section letter or number (if not part of page number)
- Page number(s)
- Medium of publication (Print)

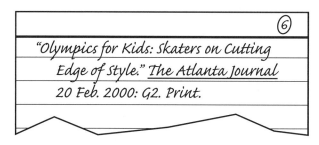

⑥

"Olympics for Kids: Skaters on Cutting Edge of Style." _The Atlanta Journal_ 20 Feb. 2000: G2. Print.

Punctuation Pointers

Place a comma between the author's last and first names.

Place a period after the author's complete name.

The title of the article is placed within quotation marks, with a period following the title inside the closing quotation marks.

The title of the magazine or newspaper is underlined or in italics.

The date is followed by a colon.

Place a period after the page number(s) and medium of publication.

- If the article begins on one page but is continued on a nonconsecutive page, put a plus sign after the first page number (e.g., 33+).

- If the article appears on consecutive pages, a hyphen is used between the page numbers (e.g., 33-36).

Documenting Electronic Sources

If you use an electronic resource instead of a print book, encyclopedia, or magazine, you must still use the appropriate format to cite your source. For example, if you reference the online version of a magazine, you should follow the format for a website.

For a website:
- Name of the author/editor(s) (if given)
- Title of article or Web page (in quotation marks)
- Name of website (underlined or in italics)
- Name of the sponsoring institution or organization (if available)
- Date of publication (day, month, and year)
- Medium of publication (Web)
- Date of your access

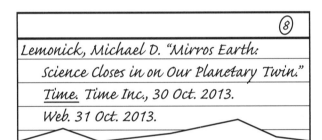

For an e-book on the Internet:
- Name of the author
- Title of book (underlined or in italics)
- Edition (if other than first edition)
- Volume number (if a multivolume work)
- Place of publication
- Name of publisher
- Year of publication
- Title of website or database from which e-book was accessed (underlined or in italics)
- Medium of publication (Web)
- Date of access

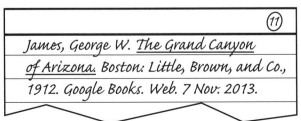

Documenting Other Sources

For an interview:
- Name of the person interviewed (last name first)
- The type of interview (e.g., telephone, personal, e-mail)
- The date of the interview (followed by a period)

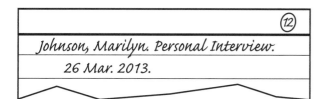

> Johnson, Marilyn. Personal Interview.
> 26 Mar. 2013. ⑫

For a film, video, or DVD:
- Film, video, or DVD title (underlined or in italics)
- The name of the director (preceded by *Dir.*)
- The name of the distributor
- The year of release
- Medium of publication (film, video, DVD)

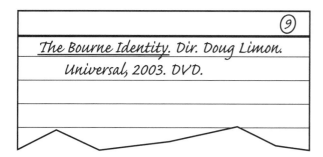

> *The Bourne Identity.* Dir. Doug Limon.
> Universal, 2003. DVD. ⑨

For a television or radio program:
- Title of episode or segment (in quotation marks)
- Title of the program (underlined or in italics)
- The network
- The local station and city (if given)
- The broadcast date
- Medium of reception (radio or television)

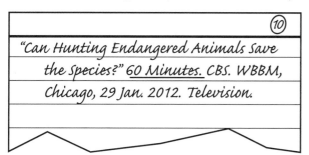

> "Can Hunting Endangered Animals Save
> the Species?" *60 Minutes.* CBS. WBBM,
> Chicago, 29 Jan. 2012. Television. ⑩

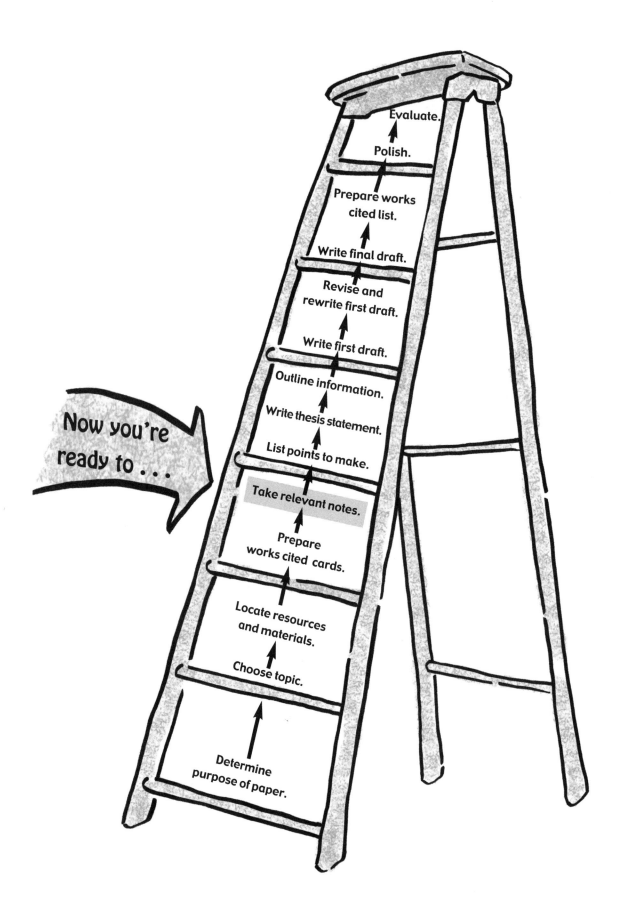

Now you're ready to . . . .

Evaluate.

Polish.

Prepare works cited list.

Write final draft.

Revise and rewrite first draft.

Write first draft.

Outline information.

Write thesis statement.

List points to make.

Take relevant notes.

Prepare works cited cards.

Locate resources and materials.

Choose topic.

Determine purpose of paper.

Taking Notes

As you discover sources and begin to read about your research topic, you will also begin the process of taking notes. Taking notes is an important part of the process of writing a research paper. Many writers decide to take notes on index cards or slips of paper, using a different card for each note.

Helpful Hints for Taking Notes

1. Write in the top left-hand corner of the card a word or phrase that summarizes the information on the note card. Write only on the front side of the note card.

2. Write the number of the works cited card you made for the source of the information in the top right-hand corner of the new note card.

3. Write the information on the note card in your own words (in other words, *paraphrase*). Write only one idea per note card. Do not write notes from two sources on the same card.

4. If you must use quoted material, write the material enclosed in quotation marks. Limit your use of direct quotes when taking notes. You want to demonstrate that you are capable of expressing ideas in your own words.

5. At the bottom of every note card, write the page number of the source from which you gathered the information.

5 Take relevant notes.

Media Events   ①

Television specials focus on U.F.O.s and ancient astronaut mysteries.

page 11

Writing Note Cards with Direct Quotations

If you come across a line, sentence, or phrase that you want to copy into your paper, place quotation marks around the borrowed material and acknowledge where you found the information. However, a good research paper will not contain much copied material because a young research scholar will instead paraphrase ideas, and then draw his or her own conclusion.

The following note card shows a direct quote. Note that the quoted material is placed within quotation marks.

> U.N. work   ③
>
> "The U.N. acts as the world's conscience, and over eighty-five percent of the work that is done by the U.N. is in the social, economic, and cultural fields."
>
> page 126

Here's How It Works

Imagine that you are writing a research paper on dinosaurs. Your main idea is that dinosaurs resembled present-day birds more than present-day reptiles. Read the excerpt below and think about what information is important to your topic.

To take notes, copy key words and phrases onto a note card. See the sample below.

> Dinosaur Appearance   4
>
> resembled birds
> · leg and foot structure
> · upright posture

For many years, people thought that dinosaurs were clumsy, slow-moving creatures that lived much like modern reptiles. However, fossil evidence shows that some kinds of dinosaurs—especially small theropods—probably were much more active than most present-day reptiles. In addition, most dinosaurs resembled birds, rather than modern reptiles, in their leg and foot structure and upright posture. Scientists generally agree that dinosaurs are closer ancestors of birds than of present-day reptiles. They believe that the study of birds can help us learn about the life of dinosaurs.

Name _____ Date _____

Read the paragraphs about life in Ancient Rome. Then take notes on the three sample cards. Each card represents a different topic.

Life in Ancient Rome

The capital and largest city of the Roman Empire was Rome. At its height, Rome had nearly one million inhabitants. Other important cities included Alexandra, Antioch, and Constantinople. These cities were centers of trade and culture. The cities were carefully planned by Roman engineers. Roman public buildings were conveniently located, and there were both sewage and water-supply systems. The forum, a large open space surrounded by markets, temples, and government buildings, was in the center of a Roman city.

The first people to live in Rome were farmers and shepherds. The Roman army was made of farmers who worked their own land. These farmers planted crops in the spring and then harvested them in the fall. They fought in the army during the summer. As Rome expanded its territory, farmers were often sent to fight abroad for extended periods of time. This meant they had to sell their land. Large estates were then built by wealthy Romans where crops and livestock were sold for a profit.

The father was the head of the Roman household. All the members of his household were under his control. The father had the power to sell his children into slavery. A son could not have legal authority over his own children or own property as long as his father was alive. For this reason many households were very large and included the families of married sons.

Ancient Rome: City Life

Ancient Rome: Rural Life

Ancient Rome: Family Life

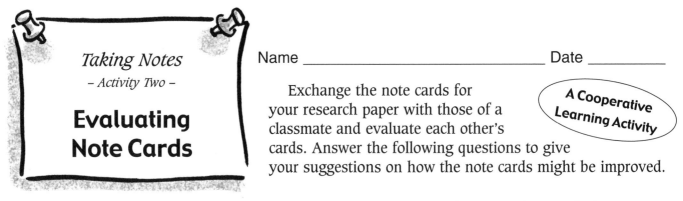

Taking Notes

– Activity Two –

Evaluating Note Cards

Name _____ Date _____

Exchange the note cards for your research paper with those of a classmate and evaluate each other's cards. Answer the following questions to give your suggestions on how the note cards might be improved.

1. Do any of your partner's note cards appear to be unrelated to the main ideas? Which ones?

   _____

   _____

2. Did you notice any cards without topic headings?

   _____

   _____

3. Do any cards have more than one idea per card? Are the ideas related or unrelated? Would you suggest making multiple cards, or would you leave the card as your classmate has arranged it? Why?

   _____

   _____

   _____

   _____

4. Have you read any cards that have used direct quotations? Were the quotations correctly punctuated?

   _____

   _____

5. What did you discover to be the most interesting thing about your classmate's notes? What was least interesting? Why?

   _____

   _____

6. After checking your partner's note cards, did you notice any misspelled words, incorrect punctuation, or omission of page numbers and source card numbers?

   _____

   _____

How to Write a Great Research Paper, Revised Edition

Organizing Your Information

Once you have chosen the topic for your research paper and have located and surveyed a number of resource materials, you are ready to list all of the points you wish to make or questions you wish to ask in the paper. When making this list, begin to think about a purpose statement or the main idea (**the thesis statement**). This main idea will be included in the introductory paragraph. You will organize your list of points into an outline.

Thesis Statement

Stating your main idea, or **thesis,** is one of the most important steps in developing your topic. It sets in motion your investigation of the facts so that you can reach an original conclusion in your paper. You may think of the thesis statement as a road map, or a guide, to take you in the right direction. For example, if your subject is dinosaurs, and your topic is Characteristics of Carnivorous Dinosaurs, a possible thesis might be: The Allosaurus and the Tyrannosaurus had big teeth and powerful claws for eating meat.

Preliminary Outline

The first (or preliminary) outline is intended to serve as a guide for writing your research paper. Begin the outline by thinking about your topic and asking yourself questions to discover the major categories (main topics) and supporting information (subtopics). Using the answers to your questions as your headings and subheadings, you may begin to write your preliminary outline.

As you begin to read through your note cards, you will encounter some irrelevant (unimportant) points. These can be eliminated. Your reading will also suggest new points that you will want to include in the paper. Therefore, keep in mind that you should revise and edit your preliminary outline as you continue to take notes.

6 List points you wish to make.

7 Write a thesis statement.

8 Outline the information you have gathered.

Think About It!

- At the top of your page, write the title of your research paper.

- Next, write Main Idea, followed by your main idea statement (your thesis statement).

- Use key words and phrases from your note cards. Organize them into topics and subtopics.

- Your first outline may be general; as you proceed you will add more detail.

You should ask yourself what the main reason is for writing your research paper. Make a list of issues that you plan to investigate.

Ask questions

List points you want to make

Write a thesis statement

Outline your information

An Example of the Process of Organizing

Tonya is a seventh grader. She wanted to learn more about the Bermuda Triangle and chose it as the topic of her research paper. She began by asking a few questions that helped in beginning her research.

1. What is the Bermuda Triangle?
2. What has happened in the Bermuda Triangle?
3. What explanations are given for these happenings?

After doing a survey of information on the Bermuda Triangle, Tonya listed the points that she wanted to make in her research paper:

- Reports of unusual happenings near the Bermuda Triangle are found in books and magazine articles.
- Television and radio talk shows have tried to explain the strange stories.
- Explanations about the area are mysterious and unresolved.

After additional research, Tonya wrote this thesis statement:

The mysterious Bermuda Triangle has received attention as the subject of books, magazine articles, and radio and television talk shows, but explanations for the unusual stories remain unknown.

Then Tonya arranged her list of topics and subtopics into a preliminary outline.

    I. The Bermuda Triangle
        A. Location
            1. 440,000 square miles
            2. Florida, Bermuda, Puerto Rico
        B. Attention received
            1. Books
            2. Magazine articles
            3. Radio and television talk shows
            4. UFOs and astronaut mysteries
        C. Explanations
            1. Outer space
            2. Disappearances
        D. Conclusion
            1. Unknown
            2. Disturbances

Some Ideas to Consider

The same research on a single topic can be interpreted in different ways. As a result, the facts and opinions found in research can support different thesis statements.

For example, after reading the following paragraph about the novel *Roll of Thunder, Hear My Cry,* you might write a number of different thesis statements.

> *Roll of Thunder, Hear My Cry* is a novel set in the back country of rural Louisiana along black and white racial boundaries during the post-Depression era. The story is told by an adolescent black girl living in a household of three generations, including her two brothers, father, mother, and grandmother. This proud family, who had bought and maintained a large farm after Reconstruction, stands to lose its farm to a nearby greedy white farmer who has threatened them with scare tactics and white power.

Here are some possible approaches for thesis statements:

Examine the teenagers' feelings: *Roll of Thunder, Hear My Cry* illustrates the feelings of African American teenagers toward the threat of racial violence.

Look at racial discrimination against African Americans: *Roll of Thunder, Hear My Cry* gives an inside look into the lives of young African Americans in a world of racial discrimination.

Explore the problems of a young African American girl growing up in a segregated society: *Roll of Thunder, Hear My Cry* addresses the issues that a young African American girl faces in her struggle for equality.

Organizing Information
– Activity One –

Practice Writing a Thesis Statement

Name _____ Date _____

Write a possible thesis statement for each research question below. Practice stating a contention or position. Because you have not completed research on the topics, your thesis statements may not be true. It is, however, important to practice wording the statements so that when you have done your research you will be able to write a succinct statement of your findings.

1. Should we save the ozone layer from destruction?

   Thesis: _____

   _____

   _____

2. Should women fight in the armed services?

   Thesis: _____

   _____

   _____

3. What can be done about teenage pregnancies?

   Thesis: _____

   _____

   _____

4. Why is the Nile River considered a cradle of civilization?

   Thesis: _____

   _____

   _____

5. How serious are the drawbacks of shoplifting?

   Thesis: _____

   _____

   _____

6. Did humankind originate in Africa?

   Thesis: _____

   _____

   _____

How to Write a Great Research Paper, Revised Edition
Copyright © 2014 World Book, Inc./Incentive Publications, Chicago, IL

Name _____ Date _____

In the space provided, write a thesis statement (main idea) for your research paper.

_____

_____

_____

_____

Check the box(es) below that apply.

☐ Is my thesis sentence the answer to a question?

☐ Is my thesis a comparison of two or more things?

☐ Is my thesis a summary of information about my subject?

☐ Is my thesis proving or disproving a principle?

Getting Feedback

Exchange and evaluate thesis statements with a classmate. After you have evaluated your classmate's thesis statement, ask yourself if you need to revise your own thesis statement.

Comments from _____.

_____

_____

_____

_____

_____

_____

_____

_____

Writing a Preliminary Outline

Outlines can follow different sets of rules, and teachers' preferences may vary.

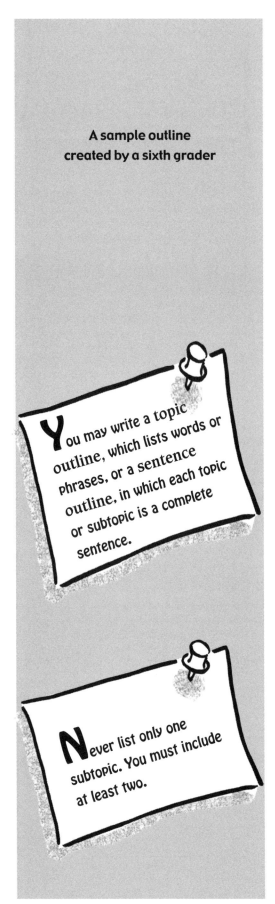

A sample outline created by a sixth grader

The Life and Times of Bo Jackson
I. Early Life
   A. Family
   B. School
II. College Years
   A. Football
   B. Track
   C. Baseball
III. Professional Sports Career
   A. Football
   B. Baseball
   C. Short Comeback
IV. Adult Life
   A. Family
   B. Sports endorsements

You may write a topic outline, which lists words or phrases, or a sentence outline, in which each topic or subtopic is a complete sentence.

Never list only one subtopic. You must include at least two.

Guidelines for Writing an Outline

1. The title of your paper goes at the top of the page.

2. Place a Roman numeral followed by a period before each main topic.
   Example: **I. Rural Life in Louisiana**

3. Subtopics are listed under the topics. Use capital letters (A, B, C, . . .) followed by periods to label subtopics. Place the letters directly underneath the first letter of the first word of the main topic.
   Example: **I. Later Years of Stardom**
      A. Later movies
      B. Retirement

4. Do not place a period after a main topic or a subtopic, unless you are writing a sentence outline.
   Example: **II. Kinds of Dinosaurs**

5. Begin the main topic and subtopic with a capital letter, and capitalize any proper nouns.

6. An outline should use parallel structure—the use of the same kind of word or phrase.
   Example: **I. Later Years of Stardom**
      A. Later movies
      B. When did she retire from movies?

This example is **incorrect** because the topic and first subtopic are written as phrases and the second subtopic is written as a complete sentence (a question). The structure is not parallel.

Name _____ Date _____

Categorize the following list into topics supported by subtopics. Then fill in the preliminary outline.

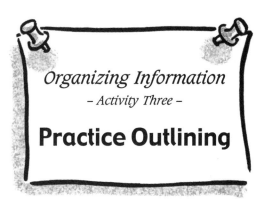
camera
post-production
film
exhibition
development
how motion pictures work
sound track
history of motion pictures
distribution
production
making motion pictures
pre-production
motion picture industry

Motion Picture Industry

I. _____

    A. _____

    B. _____

    C. _____

    D. _____

II. _____

    A. _____

    B. _____

    C. _____

III. _____

    A. _____

    B. _____

IV. _____

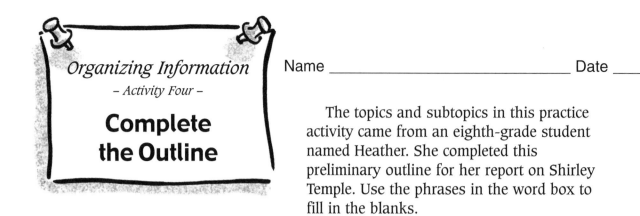

Name _____ Date _____

The topics and subtopics in this practice activity came from an eighth-grade student named Heather. She completed this preliminary outline for her report on Shirley Temple. Use the phrases in the word box to fill in the blanks.

The Lifetime Career of Shirley Temple

I. Early Years

    A. _____

    B. _____

    C. "Bojangles" Robinson

II. Later Years

    A. _____

    B. _____

III. _____

    A. Married life

    B. _____

> national positions
>
> later movies
>
> early childhood
>
> movie retirement
>
> first movies
>
> after movies

Name _____ Date _____

Test your outline knowledge. Using the scrambled information below, locate the main ideas, subtopics, and details in the list in the left column, and use them to complete the outline in the right column.

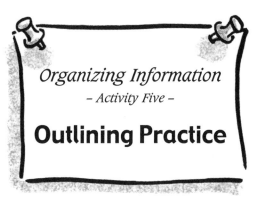

Organizing Information
– Activity Five –

Outlining Practice

verse form

first period of histories, comedies, and tragedies

his life in Stratford

sonnets of Shakespeare

vocabulary

early poems of Shakespeare

third period of great tragedies

rhetoric

first recognition of Shakespeare

composition of sonnets

criticisms of Shakespeare

work in theater companies

second period of historical drama and romantic comedies

narrative poems of Shakespeare

last years of Shakespeare

The Life and Writings of Shakespeare

I. The Life of William Shakespeare

   A. _____

   B. Early career in London

      1. _____

      2. _____

      3. _____

   C. _____

II. Plays of Shakespeare

   A. _____

   B. _____

   C. _____

   D. Fourth period of comedies and history

III. Poems of Shakespeare

   A. _____

   B. _____

      1. _____

      2. Themes of sonnets

IV. Style of Shakespeare

   A. _____

   B. _____

   C. Imagery

   D. _____

V. _____

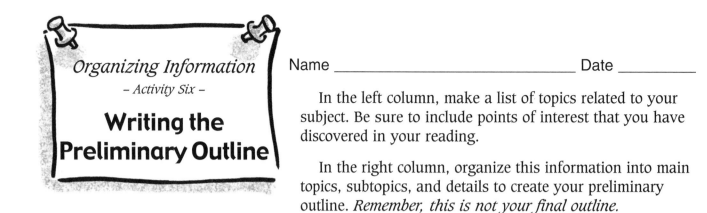

Organizing Information

– Activity Six –

Writing the Preliminary Outline

Name _____ Date _____

    In the left column, make a list of topics related to your subject. Be sure to include points of interest that you have discovered in your reading.

    In the right column, organize this information into main topics, subtopics, and details to create your preliminary outline. *Remember, this is not your final outline.*

    How to Write a Great Research Paper, Revised Edition

Name _____ Date _____

Exchange your preliminary outline with a classmate. Read the outline. Evaluate it by answering the following questions.

A Cooperative Learning Activity

1. Does the outline begin with a title of the paper?   Yes ___ No ___
   If yes, after reading the outline, do you think the title is appropriate?
   If no, what do you think the title should be?

   _____

2. What heading(s) or subheading(s) should be omitted, changed, or added to the outline?

   _____

   _____

3. Has your classmate used correct outline form to indicate subtopic(s)?   Yes ___ No ___
   If not, which subtopic(s) would you change?

   _____

   _____

4. Is any subtopic placed under the wrong main topic?   Yes ___ No ___
   If yes, name the subtopic and tell where you would place it.

   _____

5. Are all the topics and subtopics placed directly under one another
   so that all capital letters and numerals are aligned properly?   Yes ___ No ___
   If no, where would you make changes?

   _____

   _____

6. What is your overall impression of your classmate's outline?

   _____

   _____

7. Can you suggest any further improvement?

   _____

   _____

8. Are there topics that require additional research?   Yes ___ No ___
   List those topics here.

   _____

   _____

Sample Student Outlines

Review the final outline written by Major, a middle-school student in Atlanta, Georgia. Pay attention to how he organized and incorporated the guidelines for writing an outline.

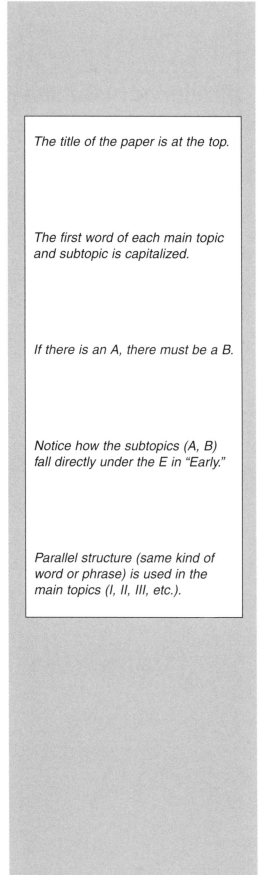

The title of the paper is at the top.

The first word of each main topic and subtopic is capitalized.

If there is an A, there must be a B.

Notice how the subtopics (A, B) fall directly under the E in "Early."

Parallel structure (same kind of word or phrase) is used in the main topics (I, II, III, etc.).

How Did Ray Charles's Music Change the History of American Music?

I. Introduction

II. History of American Music
   A. Native Americans
   B. Multi-Ethnic Population
   C. Modern Music

III. Golden Age of Music
   A. Nineteenth Century
   B. Twentieth Century

IV. Early Years of Ray Charles
   A. Childhood
   B. Blindness

V. Middle Years of Ray Charles
   A. Jazz
   B. Gospel
   C. Pop

VI. Final Years of Ray Charles
   A. Recordings
   B. Performances
   C. Death

VII. Musical Achievements of Ray Charles
   A. Grammy Awards
   B. Georgia Music Hall of Fame
   C. African Musical Award

VIII. Ray Charles: Father of Soul

The Bermuda Triangle

I. Introduction
  A. Media events
  B. No calls for help
  C. "All is well"

II. Location
  A. 440,000 square miles
  B. Florida, Bermuda, Puerto Rico

III. Legend
  A. Military crafts
  B. Christmas Winds
  C. U.S.S. Cyclops

IV. Opinions
  A. Flying saucer
  B. Disintegration

V. Conclusion
  A. Natural force
  B. Atmospheric disturbance
  C. Gravitational disturbance
  D. Electromagnetic disturbance.

This outline was written by a student named Tonya. She uses several words rather than single words for subtopics.

Shakespeare and the Globe Theater

I. William Shakespeare
  A. Early life
  B. Family
  C. Education
  D. Achievements

II. Globe Theater
  A. Plays
  B. Actors
  C. Audience
  D. Levels

III. Globe Theater Fire
  A. Burning
  B. Rebuilding

IV. Conclusion

This outline, written by a student named Frank, provides another example of correct organization, style, capitalization, and parallel structure.

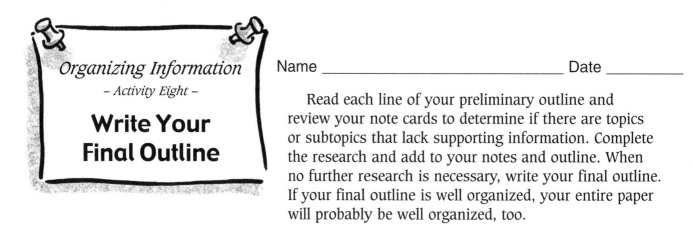

Organizing Information
– *Activity Eight* –

Write Your Final Outline

Read each line of your preliminary outline and review your note cards to determine if there are topics or subtopics that lack supporting information. Complete the research and add to your notes and outline. When no further research is necessary, write your final outline. If your final outline is well organized, your entire paper will probably be well organized, too.

Guidelines for Writing the Final Outline

1. In writing your final outline, keep in mind that you can write either a topic outline or a sentence outline. (A topic outline uses words or phrases; a sentence outline is written in complete sentences.)

2. Information should be organized logically into topics, subtopics, and details.

3. The topics and subtopics should support your thesis statement.

4. Your conclusion (often the last main topic on your outline) should summarize the main points examined in the body of the paper.

Write your final outline on the lines provided below.

_____

_____

_____

_____

_____

_____

_____

_____

_____

_____

_____

_____

_____

_____

Name _____ Date _____

Working with a classmate, read and discuss each other's outlines. Answer the following questions about your classmate's outline. Then, use your classmate's comments as you revise your own final outline.

A Cooperative Learning Activity

1. First, read the outline carefully.
   Is the outline written in topic or sentence form? Topic _____ Sentence _____
   If not properly written in either topic or sentence form, what changes should be made?

   _____

   _____

2. After reading the outline, do you detect any errors in spelling, punctuation, or capitalization?
   Yes _____ No _____ If yes, state the errors.

   _____

   _____

3. Does the outline reflect an introduction, body, and conclusion?
   Yes _____ No _____ If no, which sections need improving?

   _____

   _____

4. Are the main topics and subtopics placed directly under one another so that all capital letters and numerals are aligned? Yes _____ No _____ If no, where would you make changes?

   _____

   _____

5. Is the outline written in parallel structure (using the same kind of wording or phrasing)?
   For example, are the main topics written as nouns? in prepositional phrases? in verb phrases? in complete sentences? If not, suggest ways to revise so that the outline is parallel.

   _____

   _____

   _____

   _____

   _____

   _____

   _____

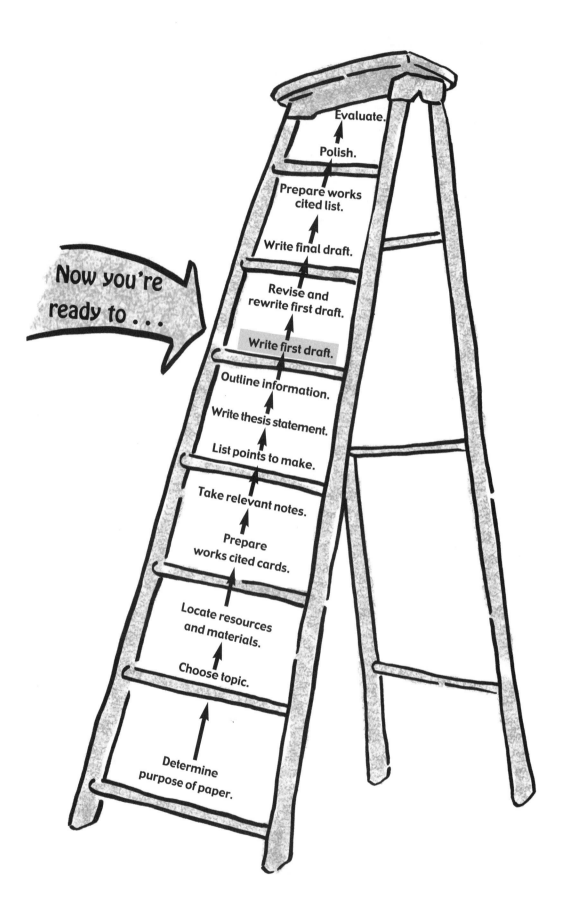

Now you're ready to . . .

Evaluate.

Polish.

Prepare works cited list.

Write final draft.

Revise and rewrite first draft.

Write first draft.

Outline information.

Write thesis statement.

List points to make.

Take relevant notes.

Prepare works cited cards.

Locate resources and materials.

Choose topic.

Determine purpose of paper.

Writing
the First Draft

With your note cards and preliminary outline prepared, you are ready to write the first draft of your research paper. As you begin, concentrate on putting down your ideas. Schedule your time wisely so that you will have time to edit your work to determine what needs to be revised or deleted.

Here are some reminders as you begin your first draft:

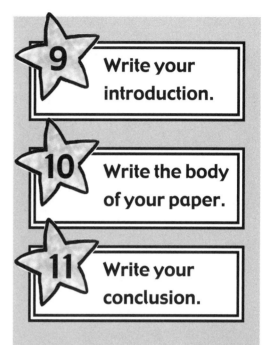

9 Write your introduction.

10 Write the body of your paper.

11 Write your conclusion.

Introduction
- The purpose of the introduction is to grab the reader's attention.
- The thesis statement (main idea) is often written as the last sentence in the introductory paragraph.
- The introduction may be one or two paragraphs long.

Body
- Before writing the body of your paper, separate your note cards according to the main topic and subtopics as shown on your outline.
- Read your note cards aloud. If you discover you have two or more note cards with similar information, place them together.
- Read the cards again to find a logical order. Turn the note cards over as you use them in your draft. Do not discard any cards, as you may be able to use them later.

Documentation
- Make sure information included in the paper is properly documented. (See pages 52 and 53 for more information on documenting information.)
- Use the MLA format of parenthetical documentation or another acceptable format (either footnotes or endnotes).
- If you use a word-for-word quotation, enclose it in quotation marks and identify the source.

Conclusion
- The conclusion signals that the paper is coming to an end. It should summarize the main ideas given in the paper.
- The conclusion may be based on your opinion and should not introduce any new information.
- The conclusion is usually one or two paragraphs long.

Giving Credit When Credit Is Due

Documentation is the process of giving credit to the sources you reference in your research paper. In the past, endnotes and footnotes were commonly used to recognize the sources and authors used in a paper. *Endnotes* are placed at the end of the paper on a separate page. *Footnotes* are written at the bottom (foot) of each page.

More recently, the most commonly accepted practice in middle schools, high schools, and colleges is to use *parenthetical documentation* (or in-text citations). In parenthetical documentation, the author's last name and the page number on which the information was found are placed within parentheses immediately following the sentence that contains the cited information. For example: (Graham 212).

Guidelines for Documenting Sources

1. As you complete your research, it is important to distinguish between information that requires in-text citations and information that does not. If information is common knowledge, you do not need to cite a source for it. For example, a statement that John F. Kennedy was elected president before Richard Nixon is common knowledge and does not need a citation.

   Here are a couple helpful guidelines:

   - If a fact is found in several encyclopedias, textbooks, or almanacs, you probably do not need to cite a specific source for that fact.

   - If you conduct surveys or make observations on your own, you do not need a citation.

2. If you quote (copy) information directly from a source, then you must place the information within quotation marks. Follow the quote with parentheses containing the author's last name and the page number on which you found the information.

"If a man does not keep pace with his companions . . . perhaps it is because he hears a different drummer." (Thoreau 124)

3. If you write information in your own words (paraphrase), and the information contains important ideas and facts you did not know, do not place the information in quotation marks. The information should be followed by the author's last name and page number within parentheses and then a period.

Since 1954, more than 50 ships and aircraft have vanished in or near the Bermuda Triangle (Burgess 208).

4. Notice that in this example there is no punctuation (comma) between the author and page number.

(Burgess 208).

5. If you use the author's name in a paraphrase or quotation, then do not place the author's name in the parentheses at the end of the sentence.

Burgess stated that since 1954 more than 50 ships and aircraft have vanished (208).

6. When there is no stated author, place the name of the source and page number within parentheses.

She was a political activist for the Republican Party (Academic American Encyclopedia 99).

7. When there are two or more authors for one work, state the last names. Separate the names with commas and use the word *and* before the final name.

(Whitting, Barry, and Harvey 125)

8. If there are more than three authors for one source, use the first author's last name, followed by *et al.* (Latin for *and others*).

(Brandes et al. 32)

9. If your sources have two or more authors with the same last name, write both the first and last name of the author in the parentheses to identify which source you are referencing.

(Robert Burgess 208)

10. If you are citing two or more works by the same author, place a comma after the last name of the author followed by the title of the work and the page reference, so that readers will know which work the citation refers to.

(Burgess, *The Bermuda Triangle* 208)

11. When you are citing a magazine article with no author given, it is permissible to shorten the title to a key word (or words) for the in-text citation. Remember, though, you must give the full title on the works cited page.

If the full title is "Artificial Hip Goes Pro With Bo," your citation may read ("Artificial Hip" 10).

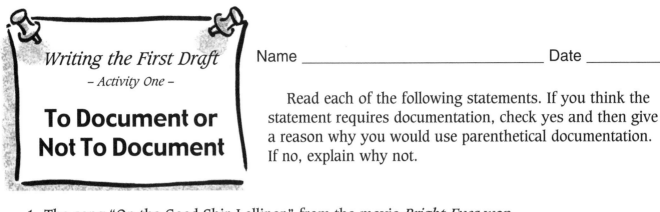

Writing the First Draft

– Activity One –

To Document or Not To Document

Name _____ Date _____

Read each of the following statements. If you think the statement requires documentation, check yes and then give a reason why you would use parenthetical documentation. If no, explain why not.

1. The song "On the Good Ship Lollipop" from the movie *Bright Eyes* won an Academy Award.　　　　　　　　　　　　　　　　　*Yes* ___ *No* ___

   _____

2. Scientists generally agree that dinosaurs are closer ancestors of birds than of present-day reptiles.　　　　　　　　　　　　　　*Yes* ___ *No* ___

   _____

3. Martin Luther King, Jr., was a famous African American civil rights leader during the 1960s.　　　　　　　　　　　　　　　　　*Yes* ___ *No* ___

   _____

4. Some North American Indians, such as the Chippewa, recorded some of their tribal songs on bark.　　　　　　　　　　　　　*Yes* ___ *No* ___

   _____

5. Nancy Kerrigan won a silver medal, and Tonya Harding placed eighth in the ice skating competition of the 1994 Winter Olympics.　*Yes* ___ *No* ___

   _____

6. The Mexican culture is a prime example of Mestizo, a blend of Native American cultures and Spanish culture.　　　　　　　　　*Yes* ___ *No* ___

   _____

Parenthetical Citations

1. Following Tonya's passage below, write the parenthetical documentation for the article "Bermuda Triangle" by Robert Burgess from page 208 of *The World Book Encyclopedia*.
   The first recorded disappearance of a U.S. ship in the Bermuda Triangle occurred in March, 1918, when the U.S.S. Cyclops vanished (_____).

2. Read the following passage written by a student named Keith. He has paraphrased information from page 10 of an article "Artificial Hip Goes Pro With Bo" (no author listed) from *Sports Illustrated*. Write the parenthetical documentation for this passage.
   After his hip replacement, Bo trained for almost a year to strengthen his leg and hip. In 1993, he returned to baseball with the Chicago White Sox (_____).

Begin with the Introduction

When writing the introductory paragraphs, keep in mind the four main purposes of an introduction. An introduction:

- explains the subject,
- provides background information,
- states the purpose of the research paper, and
- makes a thesis statement.

It is important to grab your reader's attention. Do this by:

- starting with a quotation,
- beginning with a question,
- stating a surprising or unusual fact, or
- relating the topic to personal experiences.

Read the introduction below on the Cape Hatteras Lighthouse. The paragraph was written by an eighth-grade student. Notice that in the first sentence, the writer used an interesting fact to grab the reader's attention. Also notice that the thesis statement is the last sentence in the paragraph.

> The Cape Hatteras Lighthouse, the tallest in America, has illuminated the dangerous shoals off Cape Hatteras, North Carolina, for over 116 years. It is now being threatened by the treacherous waves and erosion of the Atlantic Ocean and could be destroyed by a major storm. There are several ways in which the lighthouse can be saved. The Cape Hatteras Lighthouse should be saved so that future generations can enjoy this historical landmark.

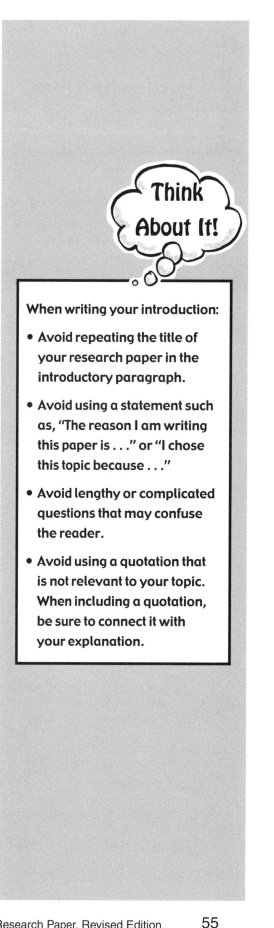

Think About It!

When writing your introduction:

- Avoid repeating the title of your research paper in the introductory paragraph.

- Avoid using a statement such as, "The reason I am writing this paper is . . ." or "I chose this topic because . . ."

- Avoid lengthy or complicated questions that may confuse the reader.

- Avoid using a quotation that is not relevant to your topic. When including a quotation, be sure to connect it with your explanation.

Writing the First Draft

– Activity Two –

Evaluating the Introduction

Name _____ Date _____

Working with a classmate, exchange, read, and discuss your introductions. Answer the following questions as you read your classmate's paragraph(s). Then use your classmate's comments to revise your introduction.

A Cooperative Learning Activity

1. Does the introduction have an attention grabber?   *Yes ___ No ___*

   If not, what changes would you suggest?

   _____

   _____

2. Does the introduction identify a specific subject?   *Yes ___ No ___*

   If not, is the subject too broad or too narrow? Explain.

   _____

   _____

   _____

3. Does the introduction provide sufficient, relevant background information?   *Yes ___ No ___*

   If not, what suggestions would you make?

   _____

   _____

   _____

4. Does the introduction identify a problem and give an explanation about how

   your research paper will examine or resolve the problem?   *Yes ___ No ___*

   If not, what changes or additions need to be made to the introductory paragraph(s)?

   _____

   _____

   _____

5. Is the thesis statement included in the introductory paragraph(s)?   *Yes ___ No ___*

   Does it explain the main idea or purpose of the paper?   *Yes ___ No ___*

How to Write a Great Research Paper, Revised Edition

Move on to the Body of Your Paper

A variety of organizational techniques may be used when writing the body of your research paper. Think about utilizing one or more of the following techniques:

- **Chronological order**
  Trace historical events and provide explanations with a sequence of events by time.

- **Compare and contrast**
  Use this technique to compare the past and the present, to show two sides of a topic, or to compare both the positive and negative aspects of an issue.

- **Cause and effect**
  Relate the consequences and causes of an event as part of the explanation.

- **Definition**
  Help your reader understand a difficult or complex subject.

- **Classification and analysis**
  Identify the reasons for and the consequences of various issues as you present information.

- **Question and answer**
  Tie your topic to the research by asking questions and providing answers.

- **Evidence from source material**
  Cite authorities on a particular subject through the use of quotations, paraphrased information, and summaries.

First, . . .
Next, . . .
Then . . .

. . . is similar to . . . in that . . .

If . . . occurs, then . . . is sure to follow.

What does . . . mean for future generations?

Using Graphics

In order to add interest to the body of your research paper, consider adding illustrations, graphs, or charts. Most computers allow you to create graphs, diagrams, charts, or illustrations. These graphics may also be imported from another source. (Be sure to cite sources both in your bibliography and in the text.) Choose graphics that will assist you in making your point more emphatically or to clarify complicated information. For example, illustrations might be used to identify a certain plant or animal that you are describing.

Graphs, charts, tables, diagrams, or other graphics should be placed as close as possible to the text they relate to. Color may be incorporated. However, dates and captions should be printed in black. If your graphic takes an entire page, be sure to reference it in the text (e.g., See line graph 1 on page 10.). Be sure to number your graphics in the text. (Tables should be numbered separately from other graphics.)

If you have numerous complex items that may distract from the flow of text in your paper, include the graphics in an appendix at the end of your paper.

Just as with any information uncovered during your research, be sure to evaluate the graphics for appropriateness, effectiveness, and validity. If you use a graphic and alter it, be sure it is done ethically. Do not attempt to mislead your readers. Accuracy is extremely important. Describe to your readers the changes that you have made. Be sure to include all relevant information and data concerning the graphic, including the source. Ask permission for use, if necessary.

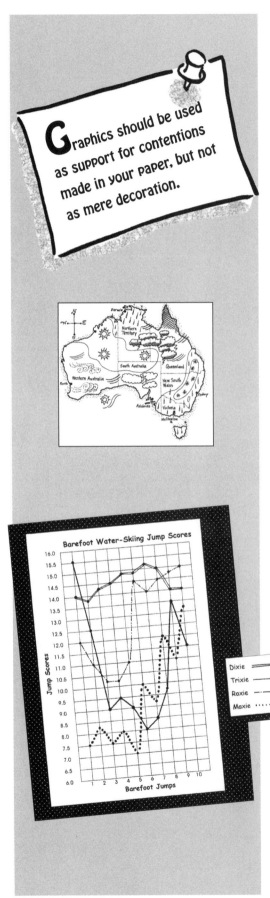

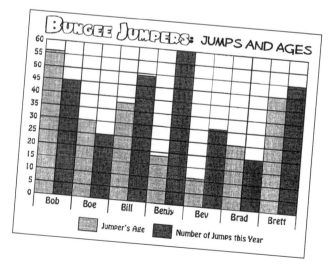

Now for the Conclusion

When writing the conclusion, restate your thesis. Point out how the thesis logically results from the analysis and discussion of points made in your research. The conclusion should also include any opinions you may have drawn based on the research and study you have done.

Summarize the main points of your research paper. Include a sentence or two that will help the reader answer the questions, "So what?" and "Does this really matter?" Be sure to support any statements you make with examples or facts. However, do not include any new information or documentation in your conclusion.

Below is a sample conclusion written by a tenth-grade student for a report on the math phenomenon of The Golden Ratio:

> How amazing is it that one simple number can shape our world so thoroughly? It is the link between the mathematical world and the human perception of perfection. The Golden Ratio continues to open doors in our understanding of life and the universe. When we think we have discovered an understanding of all the little hidden secrets of Divine Proportion, it appears and surprises us in unexpected places. For the last several thousand years, the Golden Ratio has captured the interest and wonder of humankind. Every day people are still seeking the treasures that are yet to be found in the Golden Ratio (Doran and Graham 2004).

Think About It!

Below are some of the things you can do with your conclusion:

- **Review your main ideas.**

- **Include a quotation or two to defend your position.**

- **If you are writing about a particular person, discuss his or her contributions to society.**

- **Offer suggestions for new or additional research.**

- **Discuss the facts or statistics in your research and relate them to your final statements.**

- **Challenge commonly held points of view or assumptions in order to inform the reader.**

- **Finish with a brief story that deals with the subject.**

Read these concluding paragraphs from student research papers to get ideas for incorporating the techniques listed on page 59.

The benefits of using the euro as a regional currency are summarized in this concluding paragraph:

The introduction of the euro has eased travel and commerce within Europe. Travelers used to have to exchange money at every border. Now, they can use euro coins and bills in numerous countries. Longtime residents are still adjusting to paying euro 3 instead of 41 schillings for a cup of Viennese coffee, or euro 150 instead of 300,000 lira for a pair of Italian leather shoes. But the new currency makes traveling in Europe and understanding price levels much easier for tourists and business people. Since its introduction in 2002, this regional currency has brought the countries and people of Europe closer together than ever before.

A research paper on the vaccine for chicken pox concludes with a warning that the disease still exists and can have serious consequences:

Despite the vaccine's success, there are still serious cases and even deaths from chicken pox each year. Complications are most likely to occur in unvaccinated adults who never contracted chicken pox during childhood and vulnerable populations such as infants or persons with weakened immune systems. In rare instances, even those who have been vaccinated can get the chicken pox, but these cases are normally very mild.

This summary paragraph includes a quotation that supports Ray Charles's contributions to society:

People called him "the father of soul." With his expressive playing and distinctive voice, Ray Charles combined such styles as jazz, rhythm and blues, gospel, and country. A biographer reported that Ray Charles "single-handedly changed the face of contemporary music" ("About Ray Charles"). Ray Charles broke down the color barriers within music and proved to the world that he was one of the greatest musical geniuses of the twentieth century.

Name _____ Date _____

Working with a classmate, exchange, read, and discuss each other's conclusions. Answer the following questions as you read your classmate's work. Then, use your classmate's comments to help you in revising your own.

A Cooperative Learning Activity

1. Can you locate the thesis statement?   *Yes* _____ *No* _____

   On the lines below, write your classmate's thesis statement.

   _____

   _____

2. Does the conclusion raise new issues or include new data?   *Yes* _____ *No* _____

   If yes, what new data or issues should be removed?

   _____

   _____

   _____

3. Does the conclusion give answers or interpret facts?   *Yes* _____ *No* _____

   If no, what questions are unanswered or what facts are not interpreted?

   _____

   _____

   _____

4. Does the conclusion have closure?   *Yes* _____ *No* _____

   Does it need additional information to bring closure to the research?   *Yes* _____ *No* _____

   What statements or opinions do you think would help this conclusion?

   _____

   _____

   _____

5. Does the conclusion end abruptly?   *Yes* _____ *No* _____

   Does it end in a memorable way?   *Yes* _____ *No* _____

   What might be another way to end this conclusion?

   _____

   _____

   _____

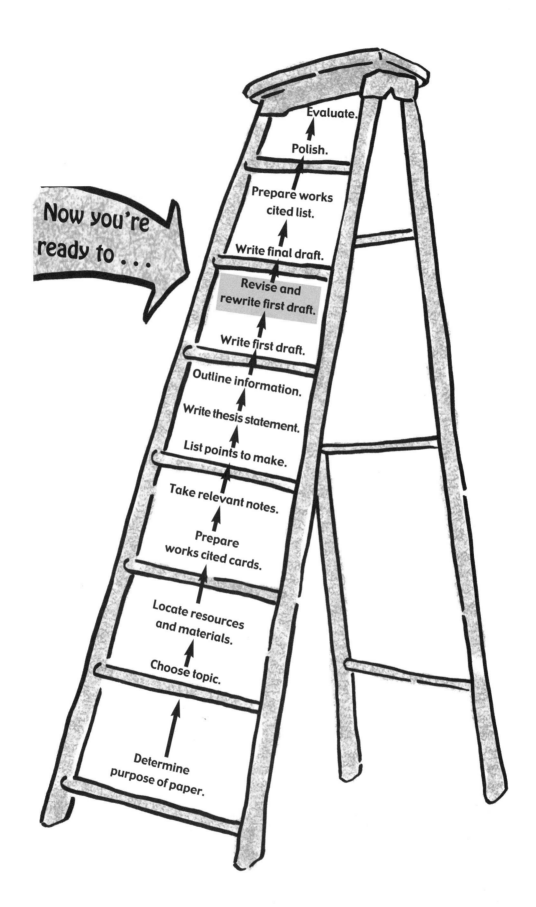

Now you're ready to . . .

Evaluate.

Polish.

Prepare works cited list.

Write final draft.

Revise and rewrite first draft.

Write first draft.

Outline information.

Write thesis statement.

List points to make.

Take relevant notes.

Prepare works cited cards.

Locate resources and materials.

Choose topic.

Determine purpose of paper.

Revising and Rewriting the First Draft

Revising and rewriting are important steps in writing a research paper, just as they are in any writing project. Regardless of how well you have planned, researched, and organized, you will need to continue making changes as you write. During this stage of writing, make any changes you feel are necessary to improve the ideas expressed in your paper.

Keep in mind that even the best writers spend time revising and editing their first drafts! It is very important to be flexible. Think of ways you can improve your selection of words and transitions, and utilize parallel structure in sentences and paragraphs.

Move through the following steps as you revise and rewrite your first draft:

1. **Let it rest for a while.**
   Why not give yourself time to write the first draft and then put it aside for a few days? During this time, you can reflect on what you have written. Students often find that after a few days, their thoughts become more organized.

2. **Develop and use a system for making corrections.**
   Mark through words, phrases, clauses, or sentences that need revising. Do not eliminate anything yet, as you may be able to use the information later.

3. **Reread your draft aloud.**
   Are there any sentences or paragraphs that sound out of place or poorly written? If so, indicate these in the margins of your paper.

4. **Grab the reader's attention.**
   Make sure that your introductory paragraph catches the reader's attention and introduces the thesis statement.

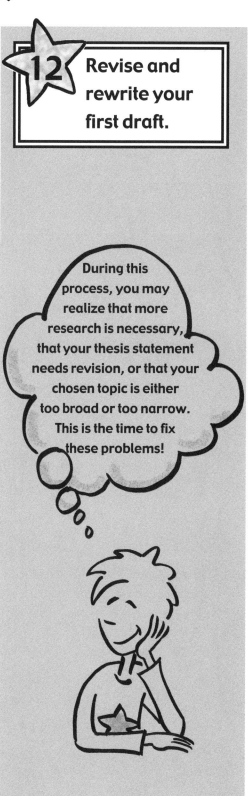

12 Revise and rewrite your first draft.

During this process, you may realize that more research is necessary, that your thesis statement needs revision, or that your chosen topic is either too broad or too narrow. This is the time to fix these problems!

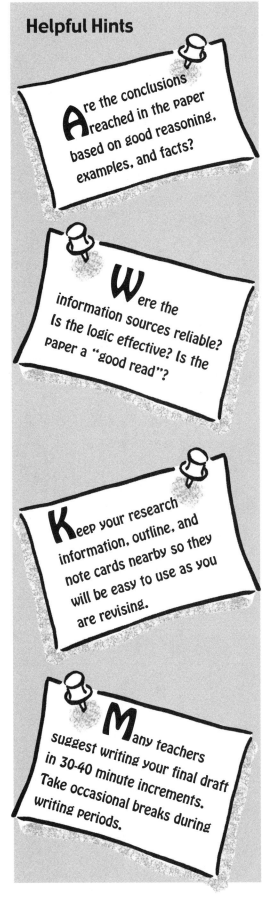

Are the conclusions reached in the paper based on good reasoning, examples, and facts?

Were the information sources reliable? Is the logic effective? Is the paper a "good read"?

Keep your research information, outline, and note cards nearby so they will be easy to use as you are revising.

Many teachers suggest writing your final draft in 30-40 minute increments. Take occasional breaks during writing periods.

5. **Make your organization easy to follow.**
   Each paragraph should contain a topic sentence with supporting details. Every supporting sentence in each paragraph should relate to its topic sentence.

6. **Check to make sure your sentences are clearly written and easy to read.**
   Add transitional words (e.g., *while, after, since, although, first, next, further, also, finally, furthermore, in addition, consequently*) to show how ideas are related to one another.

7. **Check your paper for accuracy.**
   Check punctuation, spelling, word usage, and capitalization. Consider asking a classmate, friend, parent, relative, or another teacher to assist in checking for accuracy.

8. **Be sure that your sources are properly documented.**
   If sections of the paper are not written in your own words, make sure that you have given proper credit for "borrowing" the writer's words (either quoted directly or paraphrased). Place quotation marks around another writer's exact words.

9. **Proofread your research paper carefully.**
   Your final paper should be neat and error-free. It is a good idea to proofread your paper at least three times on three different occasions.

10. **Restate your thesis in the concluding paragraph.**
    Reword your main idea for the final (restated) thesis in the concluding paragraph.

11. **Write the final copy in ink, or type it using a computer.**
    Write or type on only one side of the paper. Number the pages in the upper right-hand corner of each page, beginning with the second page.

12. **Check your final outline and add a title page.**
    Make sure you have correctly written a title page and outline according to your teacher's specifications.

Sample First Draft with Editing Marks

Frank's outline and first draft, with revisions, are shown here. As you read them, notice how he supports and develops his thesis statement. Also notice that he has carefully organized his paragraphs based on the points and details taken from his note cards.

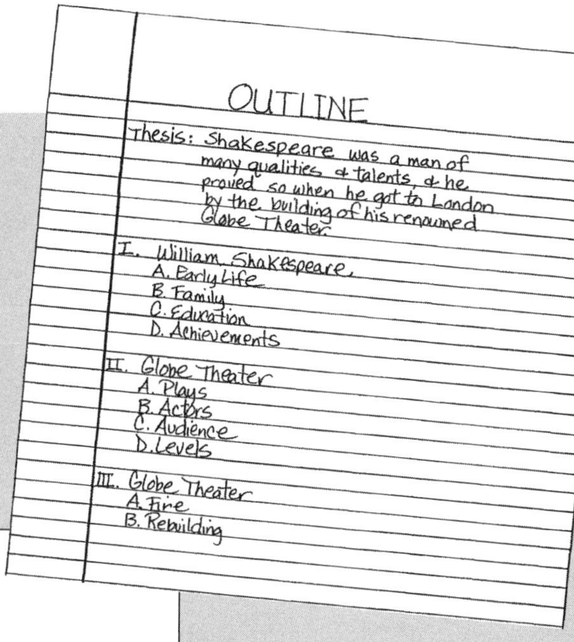

OUTLINE

Thesis: Shakespeare was a man of many qualities, & talents, & he proved so when he got to London by the building of his renowned Globe Theater.

I. William Shakespeare,
  A. Early Life
  B. Family
  C. Education
  D. Achievements

II. Globe Theater
  A. Plays
  B. Actors
  C. Audience
  D. Levels

III. Globe Theater
  A. Fire
  B. Rebuilding

and
Shakespeare ~~&~~ the Globe Theater

William Shakespeare was an English playwright. He was born in 1564 in Stratford-on-Avon, a small English town in Warwickshire. ~~He was from~~ Raised in a middle class family. He studied he attended only grammar, math, Bible, and Latin ~~in grammar school~~ grammar school where. He developed a love for poetry, and ~~playwrighting~~ wrote plays at a young age. To pursue his ~~playwrighting~~ writing dream, he left his family when he was ~~20~~ twenty, and went to London.

While in London, Shakespeare ~~developed~~ established several successful theaters. ~~which were all well attended~~. His most ~~renowned~~ famous and ~~most attended~~ popular theater was the Globe ~~Theater~~ Theatre. The Globe ~~Theater~~ Theatre opened in 1599. "Julius Caesar" was one of its first productions. Shakespeare's plays were ~~acted~~ performed by the Lord Chamberlain's men, later known as the King's Men (Comptons 2).

The Globe ~~Theater~~ Theatre had a hexagonal shape, and a court that was 55 feet across. People would crowd in around the ~~Globe~~ stage any way that they could. Sometimes, as many as 1,500 people ~~could~~ crowded into the Globe. Most people had to stand in the courtyard, but the wealthier people sat in the balconies that circled the theater. The Globe had many levels. This ~~made~~ enabled the plays to flow ~~smooth~~ smoothly, without ~~changing interruptions~~ interruptions from changing scenery.

*Write out the word **and** in the title.*

Revise sentences for smoother reading.

*Proper name uses the British spelling of **Theatre**.*

Source documented.

Improve word choice.

Reorder words for better flow.

On the first level, there was a platform stage, and an inner curtained stage flanked by two doors. At the second level, there was another curtained stage with two windows and a balcony. On the third level there was a small music gallery. Then on the roof, there was a place to fire cannons, and fly flags, as well as a crane to lower and a place where characters could be lowered by crane to the stage. (CDROM 2)

The Globe was, in fact, a great place, but had it drawbacks, too. down sports. During the first act of the play "Henry VIII" on June 29, 1613, the theater caught fire. The scene portrayed was an elaborate dance where Henry VIII first met Anne Boleyn. To produce the sounds of the this dance, Shakespeare used a combination of trumpets and music and cannon fire. Cannons had been fired from the roof before with no problem, but this time the theater-goers they weren't so lucky. After the cannon fire ignited the thatch on the South side. ignited, and In less than two hours, the whole theater burned to the ground. The Globe was later rebuilt with improvements better than before.

Shakespeare became a wealthy man as a result of the Globe Theater, and fulfilled his dream of becoming a playwright. Shakespeare wrote a total of 37 plays in his lifetime, and many of his greatest were performed at the Globe. Shakespeare died on April 23, 1616.

Name _____ Date _____

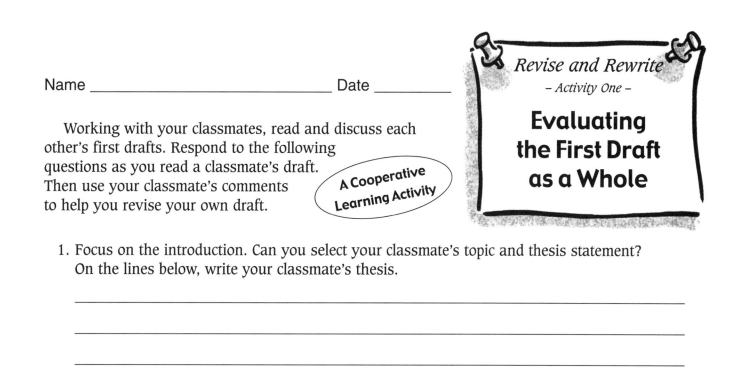

Working with your classmates, read and discuss each other's first drafts. Respond to the following questions as you read a classmate's draft. Then use your classmate's comments to help you revise your own draft.

A Cooperative Learning Activity

Revise and Rewrite
– Activity One –

Evaluating the First Draft as a Whole

1. Focus on the introduction. Can you select your classmate's topic and thesis statement? On the lines below, write your classmate's thesis.

   _____

   _____

   _____

   _____

2. Is your classmate's thesis clear? Too limited? Too broad? Do you have any suggestions for rewriting the thesis?

   _____

   _____

   _____

   _____

3. Is the introduction interesting? Did it immediately "grab your attention"? If not, suggest ways to improve the introduction.

   _____

   _____

   _____

   _____

4. Next, read the body of the draft. Write the main ideas and then locate the supporting details that accompany each idea. Point out to your classmate any main ideas that lack clear, supporting ideas.

   _____

   _____

   _____

   _____

Evaluating the First Draft as a Whole, page 2

5. After reading the first draft, what do you feel is its most fascinating aspect? Why is it fascinating? What is its least fascinating aspect? Suggest ways for improvement.

_____

_____

_____

_____

6. Are there any sentences misplaced (not in logical order)? If so, suggest a more logical order. Do the sentences flow in a rhythmic transition within the paragraphs? If not, suggest ways for improvement.

_____

_____

_____

_____

7. Has your classmate supplied enough background information? If not, what do you suggest?

_____

_____

_____

_____

8. Has your classmate documented the sources in the first draft? If not, can you detect what has been "copied" or paraphrased and what actually belongs to your classmate? If the information has been copied, is it enclosed within quotation marks?

_____

_____

_____

_____

9. Read the conclusion. Is the thesis restated?
Does the conclusion summarize the paper's main ideas?

_____

_____

_____

_____

Name _____ Date _____

When editing your introductory paragraph, keep in mind that it is important to state the reason(s) for choosing your topic and to explain what your research paper will include.

As practice, edit this first draft paragraph from a research paper titled *Does Birth Order Determine Personality?* While rewriting the paragraph, feel free to change any of the words, to place the sentences in a more logical order, and to remove any sentences that do not agree with the main topic. Also, correct any errors in spelling, capitalization, and punctuation.

I also wanted to know if my personality fits in with my birth order. this topic was chosen because I have always been intersted in Birth order and Personality Some people have really weird personalities. In this report, I will discuss what many studies prove about birth order and what many Psychologists think about birth order. Does birth order determine personality. Only children are the only children that parents give birth to. I will try to determine how well previous findings predict ones personality and also try to discover new personality traits that follow the order of one's birth.

_____

_____

_____

_____

_____

_____

_____

_____

_____

_____

_____

_____

_____

_____

Revising and Rewriting the Body of a Research Paper

Review your first draft. Consider the content of the paper and get feedback from other readers. Answer these questions:

- Does your paper have an opening that will make readers want to discover what you discovered as you were doing your research?

- Does the introduction include the main idea?

- Do you introduce the organizational technique you will use in the paper?

- Have you checked and rechecked the body of your paper to make sure that it follows your final outline?

- Is each of your main topics clearly introduced in the body of the paper?

- Have you identified the main issues of your research and provided an analysis of each issue?

- Does each of your paragraphs have a topic sentence that is sound and well written?

- Have you included evidence to support your findings?

- Are the ideas presented in a clear, sensible sequence?

- Have you used interesting language?

- Did you write a strong, summarizing conclusion?

- Did you include a citation to give credit each time you used someone else's ideas or words?

- Have you used proper documentation when quoting the work of others?

Next, proofread for conventions.
- Check for sense, fluency, and completeness of sentences.
- Check for correct grammatical construction.
- Check for correct spelling, capitalization, and punctuation.

Now you are ready to revise and rewrite! Make the changes and corrections you have determined are necessary.

When revising and rewriting the body of your research paper, you should be sure that you have developed the main topics of your outline.

Read through the following student samples and notice how they have revised their first drafts not only to fix grammar, but also to improve the organization of content. As you study the models, consider why the revisions were made.

```
              The Bermuda Triangle

                     ,which
The Bermuda Triangle∧ has received much
attention in the past few years ˣ, X̶ has
been the subject of many books,
magazine articles, and radio and
television talk shows. A television
                  the Bermuda Triangle.
special was devoted to X̶ a̶n̶d̶ i̶t̶ A̶lso,
 the Triangle
∧figures in the U.F.O. and ancient ??
astronaut mysteries. According to all
accounts, there is something very
            occurring
strange g̶o̶i̶n̶g̶ o̶n̶ out there ˣ (Kusche ˣ
L̶a̶w̶r̶e̶n̶c̶e̶ D̶a̶v̶i̶d̶ X̶ 11).

         the
In t̶h̶i̶s̶ particularly stormy and
changeable patch of ocean called the
Bermuda Triangle, ship and plane losses
                              fatal
can be sudden, surprising, and t̶o̶t̶a̶l̶.
Frequently, there are no calls for
help, no survivors, no bodies, and no
wreckage. A ship may sail into a calm
sea under a cloudless sky—then vanish.
      e
A plan∧ may disappear there, after
reporting that "All is well." X̶ bel̶ieve
t̶h̶a̶t̶ S̶ome people that have supposedly
                            have
disappeared in the Triangle h̶a̶s̶ been
        d
capture$ by countries such as Cuba ˣ
(Cusack 68).
```

Create a clause to combine sentences.

Two separate ideas are stated, but need proper transition.

*Explain the phrase **ancient astronaut mysteries**.*

Only last name of author is necessary.

Word choice is improved.

Transition is correctly used.

Check for misspelled words.

Avoid using "I believe . . ." and "I think . . ."

Only numbers whose names consist of more than one word are written as numerals.

No comma or page abbreviation is needed for this documentation.

These sentences are related and should be included in the earlier paragraph.

Add a transition between sentences.

Subject and verb must agree.

Underline the names of ships and planes.

Commercial and military craft cross this area safely every day. Since 1954, more than ~~50~~ fifty ships and aircraft~~s~~ have vanished in or near the Bermuda Triangle (Burgess~~, p.~~ 208).

Of the alleged ships and planes lost mysteriously during the last 100 years, most have met misfortune in the months of December and January. During these months ~~when~~ boreal blasts and the Christmas winds blow across the Triangle, bringing huge swells. Three of the most celebrated victims have ~~has~~ disappeared on the same date: December 5 (Gordan 75-79).

The first recorded disappearance of a U.S. ship in the Bermuda Triangle occurred in March, 1918, when the U.S.S. Cyclops vanished. On December 5, 1945, a squadron of five U.S. bombers disappeared, and a seaplane vanished while looking for the aircraft (Burgess 208).

Read the following revisions by a seventh grader. Note how the student considered both content and conventions.

The Battle of Gettysburg

During the 1850's in the U.S., the population soared in New York (Williams "July 1"). This large population increase helped the North industrialize very quickly. By the end of the decade, nearly 4/5 [four-fifths] of all factories in the U.S. and 2/3 [two-thirds] of all the rail road mileage in the U.S. were located in the North. About the same time as the North was industrializing, the South was experiencing an agricultural revolution which was fueled mainly by slaves (Williams "July 1"). On November 6, 1860, Abraham Lincoln, a moderate Republican, was elected president of the United States. Following the election, the South decided to secede from the Union. They elected Jefferson Davis, a Missouri governor, as their president. Anger quickly mounted in the North.

President Lincoln had been in office only one day when he was requested to reinforce Fort Sumter. On April 13, 1861, the Confederates bombarded and captured the fort, starting the Civil War.

On June 30, 1863, the Union Cavalry led by John Buford entered Gettysburg, Pennsylvania at about [Approximately] 11:00 AM. A brigade of Confederates had occupied the town earlier looking for shoes for their army but left realizing that the Cavalry was nearby. General Robert E. Lee, head of the army of Northern Virginia, was notified. Lee reacted quickly, converging all his forces in the small, quiet town of Gettysburg (Clark 1985). Lee sent General Heth's division to occupy Gettysburg a little ways ahead of the rest of the army of Northern Virginia. How did these two huge armies exist in come to bear on the tiny farming town of Gettysburg? What was the effect of the first two days of fighting on the outcome of the Battle of Gettysburg?

Introductory paragraph lacks thesis sentence.

Fractions should be written as words.

Start new paragraph.

Add missing space.

Paragraphs lack organization and structure. Combine paragraphs two and three.

Change sentence structure.

Improve word choice.

Capitalize proper noun.	**O** ~~I~~n the morning of July 1~~st~~, General Heth's Confederate**s** reached Herr Ridge and surveyed the approach to Gettysburg. Observing little resistance, Heth ordered his two brigades to march southeast along **C**hambersburg Pike and occupied Gettysburg (Clark).
Check punctuation. *Correct verb tense.*	Unknown to General Heth**,** General Buford's Cavalry occupied the town with two brigades. The battle ~~begins~~ *began* when one of the Union brigades was attacked by a Confederate infantry brigade. The Union brigade held their position for one hour, but eventually they were forced to retreat (Williams "July 1").
North *should not be capitalized.* *Break up run-on sentence.*	Fighting continued down Herr Ridge, across Willoughby Run, and up McPherson's Ridge. A division commander saw that he was being outflanked and ordered three regiments **n**orth of his position to retreat and reform along Seminary Ridge. Unfortunately, the messenger was killed and unable to deliver the order**.** **B**~~b~~ecause of the death of the messenger, regiments along the railroad received heavy casualties and *were* ~~was~~ then forced to retreat (Williams, "July 1").
Fix redundant wording. *Correct spelling.*	The Union brigade charged the Confederates and forced them to retreat ~~back~~ to the unfinished rail line. Half of the Confederates were taken prisoner while the remainder retreated. The Confederates were forced to change ~~there~~ *their* approach to Gettysburg. Fighting continued throughout the day with the Confederates claiming victory by day's end.
Correct verb tense. *Capitalize proper noun.* *Improve word choice.*	The second day of fighting, July 2, ~~begins~~ *began* with General Meade ordering soldiers to take position**s** along Cemetery Ridge. When the soldiers arrived, they realized that a peach orchard which stood about one-half mile to the west offered a better position. However, these **U**~~u~~nion soldiers ~~ran up against~~ *encountered* a large force heading for the same position (Clark).

How to Write a Great Research Paper, Revised Edition

Name _____ Date _____

Practice editing the following first draft paragraph written by a ninth grader. As you rewrite the paragraph, feel free to change any of the words, to place the sentences in a more logical order, and to remove any sentences that do not agree with the main topic. Also, correct any errors in spelling, capitalization, and punctuation. The title of the paper is *Heart Attacks: Causes, Prevention, and Treatments*.

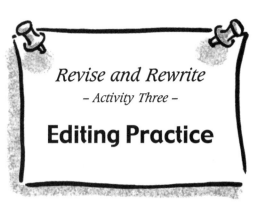

Revise and Rewrite
– Activity Three –

Editing Practice

A heart attack refers, to when a blood clot blocks the flow of one or more of your coronary artaries. When the blood flow is cut of the cells do not recieve the oxygen that they need this causes the blood supply to an area of the muscle to be cut off causing this portion of the muscle to dye (Mayo Clinic 45). Men in thier forties are more likely to have a heart attach than women? The seriousness of this depends on where the blockage occurs ("Heart Attack" 62).

_____

_____

_____

_____

_____

_____

_____

_____

_____

_____

_____

_____

_____

_____

_____

_____

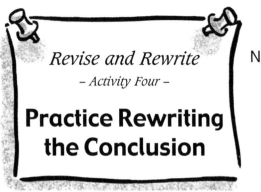

Revise and Rewrite

– Activity Four –

Practice Rewriting the Conclusion

Name _____ Date _____

Remember that the concluding paragraph(s) should restate the thesis and should include any opinions of the writer based on the research and study described in the report. Read the following conclusion written by a seventh grader. Feel free to change any of the words, to place the sentences in a more logical order, and to remove any sentences that do not agree with the main topic. Also, correct any errors in spelling, capitalization, and punctuation. If necessary, use additional paper.

In the Middle Ages parents began selling and apprenticing their children for money. In the 1600's and 1700's British employers hired children to work in factories because of a labor shortage these children worked in unhealthy environments, were given little food, and were mistreated in a variety of ways. In cities like New York, children were sent by their parents to earn money. The Fair Standards labor act was passed in 1938. This law required employers to pay children a minimum wage. It also limited a age of working children to 16 and over, and eighteen if the job is dangerous. In my opinion, child labor is unfair and unjust. Today, in Asia, most children in factories and agriculture. In Africa most of the children work as servents or they work on commercial plantations. Children in latin america mainly work in small mining operations where they have to dig and work in small tunnels that most adults cannot fit into. Europe doesn't really have a problem with children working, but it is needs to be careful with children in the Eastern and Southern parts because of this economic problems in those areas. In America most of the problems are in the southern parts along the Mexican border where companies hire illegal immigrants and their children. Child labor first became an issue in the United States in 1850's.

_____

_____

_____

_____

_____

_____

_____

_____

_____

_____

_____

_____

_____

Writing the Final Draft

The time has arrived to write your final draft. How should you proceed? You may write your paper by hand or on a computer, depending on your teacher's instructions. Just remember, your final paper should be neat as well as complete.

Proofreading at this stage is crucial because you are able to check your paper one last time for organization, clarity, parallel structure, word choice, spelling, and punctuation. Listed below are some helpful guidelines you can follow when preparing your final draft. However, pay close attention to your teacher's specific instructions for organization, style, and formatting.

- If you are handwriting your paper, use lined paper and black or blue ink.

- Double-space if you are typing your paper.

- Indent one inch for the top, left, right, and bottom margins for both handwritten and typed papers.

- Always indent the beginning of each paragraph.

- Prepare a title page that includes the title of your paper, your name, the date, and any other information the teacher requires.

- Include a complete works cited list.

- Organize your paper in this order: title page, outline, body, works cited list.

- Number the pages of your research paper beginning with the second page of the body. The first page is not numbered.

- Do not discard any materials (cards, outlines, and drafts) as you may be asked to turn these in to your teacher.

13 Write your final draft.

Check with your teacher. Are there any special requirements that you need to include?

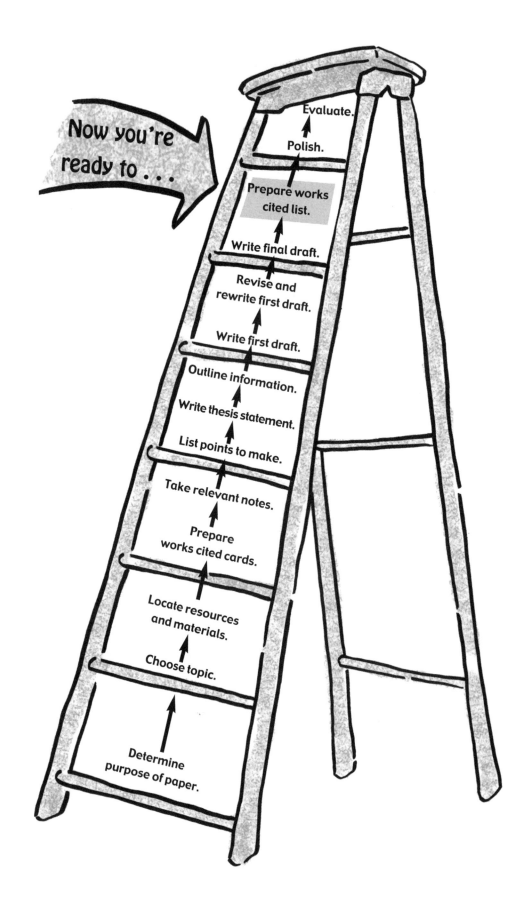

Now you're ready to . . .

Evaluate.

Polish.

Prepare works cited list.

Write final draft.

Revise and rewrite first draft.

Write first draft.

Outline information.

Write thesis statement.

List points to make.

Take relevant notes.

Prepare works cited cards.

Locate resources and materials.

Choose topic.

Determine purpose of paper.

Preparing a Works Cited List

A page at the end of your research paper should list the sources (books, encyclopedia articles, websites, magazine articles, newspaper articles, atlases, films, television programs, and so on) that you used in writing your research paper.

Because you have already made a works cited card for each of your sources, follow these steps to prepare your final list:

1. Alphabetize the cards by authors' last names. If the source does not include an author, use the first word in the title for that card.

2. Following the appropriate format for documentation, record the entries on a single sheet of paper.

Look over the sample works cited list below. Notice that the second and subsequent lines of the entries are indented.

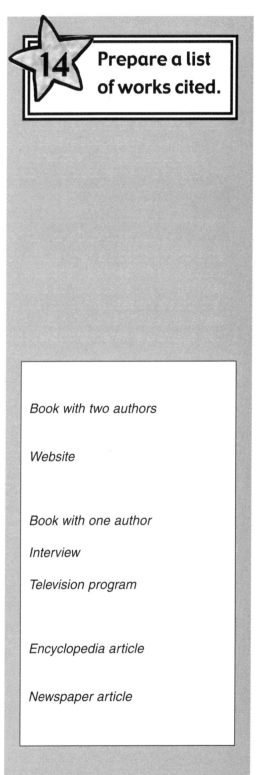

14 Prepare a list of works cited.

Fastovsky, David E., and David B. Weishampel. *Dinosaurs: A Concise Natural History.* 2nd ed. Cambridge: Cambridge University Press, 2012. Print.

Gibbons, Ann. "Did All Dinosaurs Have Feathers?" *Smithsonian.com.* Smithsonian Media, 5 July 2012. Web. 31 Oct. 2013.

Hanson, Thor. *Feathers: The Evolution of a Natural Miracle.* New York: Basic Books, 2011. Print.

Johnson, Marilyn. Personal Interview. 26 Mar. 2013.

"The 'missing link' between dinosaurs and birds?" *CBS Evening News.* CBS. WBBM, Chicago, 12 Apr. 2012. Television.

Weishampel, David B. "Dinosaur." *The World Book Encyclopedia.* 2013 ed. Print.

Wilford, John Noble. "Birdlike Dinosaur Fossil May Shake Up the Avian Family Tree." *New York Times* 02 Aug. 2011: D3. Print.

Book with two authors

Website

Book with one author

Interview

Television program

Encyclopedia article

Newspaper article

Sample Research Papers

The pages that follow show final research papers written by students. They provide helpful examples, but be sure to follow your teacher's specific instructions when preparing your own paper.

The title page, which may or may not be a required part of your research paper, usually contains the title of the research paper, the author's name, the date of the paper, and sometimes the teacher's name, school name, or course name.

Title IX: Where Are We Now?

[Author's Name]

[Teacher's Name]
[School / Course]
[Date]

Title IX: Where Are We Now?

I. Pre-Title IX

   A. Opportunities

      1. Sports

      2. Scholarships

   B. Graduation rates

      1. Pregnancy rates

      2. Test scores

      3. Graduate degrees

   C. Self-esteem

II. Post-Title IX

   A. Opportunities

      1. Sports

      2. Scholarships

   B. Graduation rates

      1. Pregnancy rates

      2. Test scores

      3. Graduate degrees

   C. Self-esteem

III. DeKalb County School Survey

IV. Conclusion

Note the use of parallel structure in the main topics and subtopics.

Also notice how all of the main topics and subtopics are correctly aligned.

Title IX: Where Are We Now?
The Body

Title IX: Where Are We Now?

Ask yourself these questions as you read this report.

- **Is the thesis clearly stated?**

- **Are the margins in keeping with your teacher's guidelines?**

- **Do the transitions help the reader to make connections and read the paper easily?**

- **Is the parenthetical documentation written and punctuated correctly?**

Title IX is a civil rights law which was designed to end discrimination against women. It states that "no person in the United States shall, on the basis of sex, be excluded from participation in, be denied the benefits of, or be subjected to discrimination under any education program or activity receiving Federal financial assistance" (Riley). Title IX was passed in 1972 and has several parts. The most well known part of Title IX allows girls to have more opportunities to play sports. However, Title IX also provides "access to Higher Education, Career Education, Education for Pregnant and Parenting Students, Employment, Learning Environment, Math and Science, Sexual Harassment, Standardized Testing and Technology" (*Title IX: I Exercise My Rights*).

Before Title IX, women didn't have the opportunity to play many sports. Donna Lopiano, the Executive Director of the Women's Sports Foundation, said, "I never forgot what it felt like to be prevented from playing Little League. Although I didn't vow to change things at the time, it does result in your developing a social justice mind-set" (Kilmeade 284-287). Many people believed that girls did not want to play sports. In 1971, only one out of every 27 girls played a varsity sport in high school. By 2002, that number had increased to one out of every 2.5 girls. Some sports that women weren't allowed to participate in were rugby, lacrosse, soccer, ice hockey, and wrestling. Now girls are allowed to play those sports and more. In 2000, over 1,600 girls played high school football, 3,000 wrestled and 1,600 played baseball (Women's Sports Foundation). Companies are starting to realize that women make buying decisions and are aiming their advertising and products at girls. Some examples are pink helmets, purple bats and princess soccer balls.

The graduation rate for girls prior to Title IX was 76.6% (Mortenson). Now a lot more girls are playing sports and they are graduating. In 1992, eighty-seven

How to Write a Great Research Paper, Revised Edition
Copyright © 2014 World Book, Inc./Incentive Publications, Chicago, IL

Title IX: Where Are We Now?
The Body (page 2)

percent of women finished high school. In 1973, forty-three percent of women registered for college. By 1994, sixty-three percent of women registered for college. Only eighteen percent of women compared to twenty-six percent of men completed all four years of college in 1971, but the numbers were equal at twenty-seven percent by 1994 (Riley). Girls who didn't play sports were more likely to smoke, drink, try drugs, drop out of school, become pregnant and they were more likely to become depressed. From 1980 to 1990 high school dropout rates for girls declined 30 percent. Girls who play a sport are about 50% less likely to become pregnant (Women's Sports Foundation). Title IX provided programs to keep pregnant teenagers and parents in school. Opportunities in science and math also increased for women.

After Title IX, scholarships also increased for women. Title IX is trying to make it that the amount of money going to each scholarship is equal. Athletic scholarships allow students who may not have been able to afford college the chance to obtain a college degree. There has been a huge jump in percentage of women getting degrees; from 1970 to 1990 the percentage has almost doubled. In 1994, men and women received equal numbers of bachelor's degrees.

Another privilege women didn't have was graduate degrees. Before Title IX women weren't getting a lot of masters, law, dental, medical, and doctoral degrees. They weren't getting very many degrees because most of the schools were limiting how many women would be allowed at that school for different degrees. Most schools limited it for fifteen or less girls at each school for medical or law degrees (Riley). When my grandmother graduated from medical school only eight percent of her class was women.

- **Facts and statistics in support of the topic sentence**

- **Varied sentence structure and clear organization**

- **Well-organized paragraphs**

Title IX: Where Are We Now?
The Body (page 3)

3

Twenty-five years later, when my mother graduated from the same medical school, 30% of her class was women.

• **Effective quotation**

Title IX helped increase women's confidence and self esteem. Playing sports raises a girl's confidence. Playing sports also makes her self images and physical health stronger. Laurie Dhue, a Television Anchor and Reporter, said, "Sports instilled in me confidence and discipline I still carry with me to this day. It also taught me time management and the concept of team, as well as a sense of competition that I have never lost." According to Lopiano, "Sport has been one of the most important socio-cultural learning experiences for boys and men for many years ... Sport is where boys have traditionally learned about teamwork, goal-setting, the pursuit of excellence in performance, and other achievement-oriental behaviors—critical skills for success in the workplace. In this economic environment, the equality of our children's lives will be dependent on two-income families. So both parents should have the advantage of experiences in sport" (Kilmeade 289-290). In 1988, a poll of women leaders of Fortune 500 companies found that eighty percent had played sports (Women's Sports Foundation). Title IX changed how people act. Because of laws like Title IX when girls grow up, they will have a good impression of themselves and they will think they are strong and capable of doing anything they want. Although Title IX has had a great impact on

• **Appropriate use of "Although"**

women, both on and off the playing fields, there are still opportunities to improve. The proportion of girls participating in sports is still less than boys. In 2000, forty percent of high school athletes were girls and forty-one percent of college athletes despite the ratio of girls to boy students being about 50/50 (Women's Sports Foundation). Boys still receive more scholarship money. Girls get about thirty-two percent of money

Title IX: Where Are We Now?
The Body (page 4)

4

spent on recruiting (137 million dollars less than the boys) (*Title IX: I Exercise My Rights*). Women still earn less compared to men and have lower level jobs. Most principals are men (65%), even though most teachers (65%) are women (*Title IX: I Exercise My Rights*). Most coaching jobs and advertising dollars are spent on men (Women's Sports Foundation).

During our research we observed many things about schools and sports. At Henderson Middle School many people play sports, but more boys than girls participate. At this school there are 15 boys and 15 girls that play basketball. There are also 24 girls and 28 boys for track and field. However, there are only 19 girl cheerleaders and at the same time, 46 boy football players. So, in total 58 girls participate in sports and 89 boys who participate in sports at Henderson Middle School ("Athletics"). As you can see, there are many more boys than girls playing sports. Also, cheerleading is not considered a sport unless they compete and at Henderson there is no competition. Therefore, by the Title IX definition, only 39 girls participate in a sport compared with 89 boys. Henderson Middle School is, therefore, not compliant with Title IX in this area. Henderson also violates Title IX in that the girl's basketball games are always at five o'clock at night and the boy's games are at seven o'clock. This violates Title IX because the parents are less likely to be able to attend the five o'clock games. All schools are supposed to have a compliance officer to ensure that the school is following Title IX rules. Henderson does not have someone who is doing this. Henderson Middle is compliant with Title IX in several ways. Henderson Middle School has locker rooms for each sex, equipment that is equal for each sports team, physical education provided for both genders and boys and girls are able to have the same core subjects. We were not able to obtain information on the numbers of students from other middle schools in Dekalb County who participate in sports, but from observation at athletic events, the

- **Relevant supporting facts**

- **Effective transitions**

- **Parenthetical documentation written correctly**

Title IX: Where Are We Now?
The Body (page 5)

numbers do not appear to differ from Henderson's.

In conclusion, Title IX has made a big change in people's lives. We have gone far to accomplish Title IX, but we still have a way to go before girls and boys are treated equally. Title IX is trying to make sure men and women are being treated equally. It ensures that programs and activities that receive money from the federal government do not discriminate on the basis of a person's sex. One of our mothers explained to us that when she was our age (twelve), she really wanted to play Little League Baseball like her brothers, but she couldn't She wasn't allowed to play because she was a girl. Title IX changed that for us. We have more opportunities to play sports. However, the opportunity for girls to play sports in Dekalb County is still less than the opportunity the boys have. The Dekalb County School System·has not really followed Title IX, but there are things that they can change to make them more compliant. They can appoint a compliance officer, change the game schedules, and provide more sports so that girls will have the same opportunities as the boys. So in all, Title IX has made a big difference, but we still have a way to go until women and men are treated equally and have the same opportunities.

- **Has the author restated the thesis?**

Title IX: Where Are We Now?
Works Cited

Works Cited

"Athletics." *DeKalb County School District*. DeKalb County Board of Education, 2009. Web. 12 Oct. 2009.

Kilmeade, Brian. *The Games Do Count: America's Best and Brightest on the Power of Sports*. New York: ReganBooks, 2004. Print.

Mortenson, Tom. "Fact Sheet: What's Wrong with the Guys?" *Postsecondary Education OPPORTUNITY*. Postsecondary Education Opportunity, 9 Aug. 2003. Web. 22 Oct. 2009.

Riley, Richard. *Title IX: 25 Years of Progress*. Washington, D.C.: U.S. Dept. of Education, 1997. Web. 23 Oct. 2009.

Title IX: I Exercise My Rights. Margaret Fund, 2006. Web. 23 Oct. 2009.

Women's Sports Foundation. "Women's Sports Facts." *University of Delaware*. University of Delaware, 15 Jan. 2002. Web. 25 Oct. 2009.

- The phrase "Works Cited" is capitalized and centered.

- The entries are alphabetized.

- The second and subsequent lines of each entry are properly indented.

Student Sample Two

**Where's
My Rattle?**
**Defensive Strategies
of Hognose Snakes**

- The paper's title is centered across the top of the page.

- The author's name and other required information also is centered.

Where's My Rattle?
Defensive Strategies of
Hognose Snakes

[Author's Name]

[Teacher's Name]
[School / Course]
[Date]

Where's My Rattle?

Defensive Strategies of Hognose Snakes

    I. Roundup of rattlesnakes

       A. Catching snakes

          1. Digging holes

          2. Pumping gas

       B. Harming environment

          1. Reducing population

          2. Lowering health

          3. Impacting ecosystem

   II. Purpose of rattles

       A. Warning predators

       B. Preventing strikes

 III. Characteristics of hognose snakes

       A. Imitating rattlesnakes

       B. Playing dead

 IV. Experiments with hognose snakes

   V. Results of experimentation

- **Each main topic and subtopic is properly capitalized and aligned.**

- **The subtopics (A, B) are lined up directly beneath the letter R in "Roundup."**

- **The outline uses parallel structure in main topics and subtopics.**

Where's My Rattle?
The Body

- **Proper use of spacing and margins**

- **Facts to support topic sentence**

- **Sentence variety**

- **Correct parenthetical documentation**

Where's My Rattle? Defensive Strategies of Hognose Snakes

Rattlesnake meat was first canned in March of 1931 by George Kenneth End of Arcadia, Florida. It was served at the Hillsboro Hotel in Tampa on April 9th of that same year (Kane 259). Since then, rattlesnakes have been used for many different purposes, one of the most common of these being rattlesnake roundups. Every year, a few dozen hunters collect between three and six hundred rattlesnakes in Georgia. The vast majority of these are Eastern Diamondbacks, although many Timber rattlesnakes are collected as well (Jensen). They are caught by one of two methods: digging through tortoise holes in order to find them or pumping gas into the holes through a hose in an effort to flush them out (Jensen). Cash prizes are awarded to hunters or teams based on length, quantity, and other distinguishing features, and the snakes are slaughtered to be used in leather products (Jensen). Along with the roundup comes a festival, and tens of thousands of people attend to see the attractions (Jensen), such as snake-handling demonstrations, snake hunts, venom-milking, and rattlesnake meat (Mealer). Human actions have a major impact on the natural behavior patterns of snakes.

Although rattlesnake roundups originally took place as an effort to lower the number of venomous snakes in areas where they could be potentially harmful to humans (Jensen), they are now highly controversial. While it is true that they "provide a local economic boost, support charitable organizations, and contribute venom for medical research" (Jensen), it is also true that they have an extremely negative impact on the environment, and they can be very dangerous. Over the last several years, there has been a major drop in the number of Eastern diamondback rattlesnakes, and many environmentalists believe that roundups are to blame (Jensen). When a population experiences significant drops in number, factors often work against them, including a

Where's My Rattle?
The Body (page 2)

lowering in the population's general health and an increase in reproduction problems (Stuart). Each species has a niche, and when one is lost or harmed, it can greatly impact the entire ecosystem. Without rattlesnakes, their food source, rodents, would have a massive population increase, which would throw the entire ecosystem out of balance. Besides all that, the nature of rattlesnake roundups forces the snakes into a type of natural selection. As the ones that rattle are being found, collected, and killed, the surviving snakes are ceasing to use their rattles. The original intended use of a snake's rattle is to warn predators away so that the snake is not forced to attack. However, without the rattle they are much more difficult to find, and they are easy to stumble upon without realizing it. Instead of scaring people off as they are supposed to, the rattlesnakes are beginning to move to their next method of defense: striking. An Eastern diamondback rattlesnake is extremely venomous, and "When they bite, the entire area around it burns like you just put a cigarette out on yourself .. Every time your heart beats after that, the venom tears up any tissue it touches," as quoted by Bill Ransberger, a man who has been bitten by rattlesnakes forty-two times while working at rattlesnake roundups (Mealer).

Experiments are being performed in an effort to discover exactly whether or not the rattlesnake roundups are permanently changing the defensive strategies of snakes. This idea works very well with the Western hognose snake, which also has extremely unique defensive characteristics. They are non-venomous snakes from the genus *Heterodon* and the family Colubridae ("Hognose Snake," *Academic American*) who live mostly in the Western area of the United States, mainly in sandy or highland areas, such as South Dakota (Birch). They are tan, brown, yellow, and black with irregular spots on their backs, and they grow to a length of twelve to

- **Has the author used sentence variety and appropriate word choice in this paragraph?**

- **Does the use of quoted material seem appropriate?**

Where's My Rattle?
The Body (page 3)

forty-eight inches and a width of two to four inches (Birch). They are often called "puff-adders" because when threatened they fill themselves with air in order to look larger, flatten their heads, and exhale loudly to make a hissing noise meant to imitate the sound of a rattlesnake (Birch). If that fails, they strike repeatedly with a closed mouth. If all of that fails, then they flip over, open their mouths, and play dead ("Hognose Snake," *Academic American*).

Western hognose snakes are perfect for adaptive behavior experiments for many reasons. First, their hiss is actually the mimicking of a rattlesnake, so the desired effect is identical. Therefore, if the hiss does not work, they are in the same predicament as the rattlesnake (Birch). Second, they fill much the same niche as a rattlesnake. They are a key component to keeping the rodent population under control in South Dakota (Birch), so if there were to be a sudden decrease in the hognose snake population, it would have the same drastic affect. There has also been research already done on the Western hognose snake's reaction to human interaction done by Burghardt and Greene in 1988 (McGuffrey). The snakes were placed alone in containers, and at ten minute intervals they were touched, stroked, then gently lifted and shook. The recovery was observed through a camera located within a stuffed owl one meter away. The experiment was repeated the next day, once with a human staring directly at the snake, once with a human standing near-by but looking away, and once with a human crouched out of sight of the snake. The snake with the human staring at it had the longest recovery time (McGuffrey). This goes to show that even the slightest human action of just looking at a snake can cause behavior changes, meaning that there is a high likelihood that the presence of humans will alter the defensive habits.

- **Use of transitional "Therefore" is helpful.**

- **Paragraph is well organized.**

Where's My Rattle?
Works Cited

Works Cited

Birch, Frank. "Western Hognose Snake (Heterodon Nasicus)." *Northern State University*. South Dakota Board of Regents, 1997. Web. 5 Oct. 2009.

"Hognose Snake." *Academic American Encyclopedia.* 1995 ed. Print.

Jensen, John. "Rattlesnake Roundups." *New Georgia Encyclopedia*. Georgia Humanities Council, 26 Mar. 2005. Web. 10 May 2009.

Kane, Joseph Nathan, Steven Anzovin, and Janet Podell. *Famous First Facts*. New York: H.W. Wilson, 1997. Print.

McGuffey, Seana. "Context Dependent Learning Using Aversive Stimuli in Eastern and Western Hognose Snakes." *Sweet Briar College*. Sweet Briar College, 2005. Web. 5 Oct. 2009.

Mealer, Bryan. "Jawboning with Snakeburger." *Salon*. Salon Media Group, 11 Mar. 2011. Web. 3 Oct. 2009.

Stuart, Simon. "Species: Unprecedented Extinction Rate, and It's Increasing 1999." *IUCN*. International Union for Conservation of Nature and Natural Resources, 1999. Web. 10 Oct. 2009.

- Works cited are alphabetized by the authors' last names, or by title if an author's name is not available.

- Online sources are correctly listed.

- Commas, periods, and colons are correctly placed.

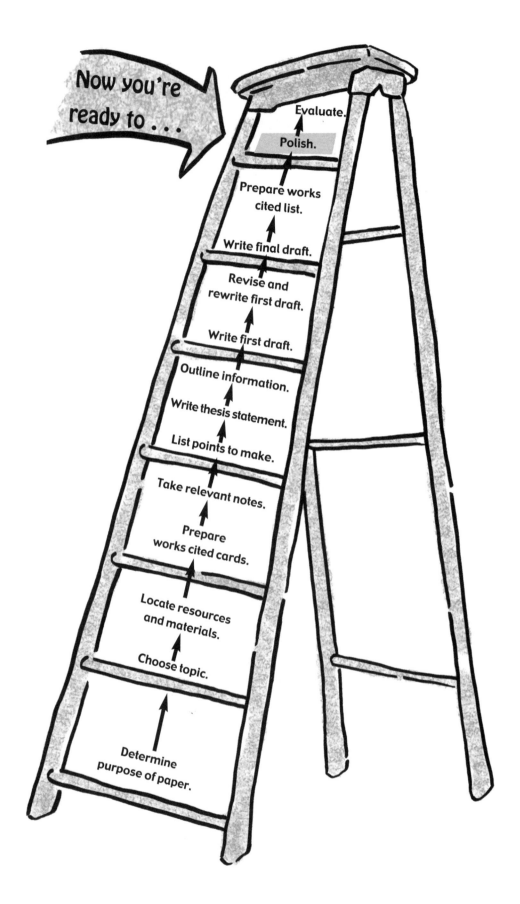

Now you're ready to . . .

Evaluate.

Polish.

Prepare works cited list.

Write final draft.

Revise and rewrite first draft.

Write first draft.

Outline information.

Write thesis statement.

List points to make.

Take relevant notes.

Prepare works cited cards.

Locate resources and materials.

Choose topic.

Determine purpose of paper.

How to Write a Great Research Paper, Revised Edition

Polishing and Evaluating

Attention to Detail Pays Off

After you have finished writing your final research paper, and before you turn it in to your teacher, carefully proofread the paper. Remember that YOU ARE TOTALLY RESPONSIBLE for any mistakes in your paper. Use the points below as a polishing checklist:

- [ ] I have carefully proofread my entire research paper and made necessary corrections.

- [ ] I have numbered each page beginning with page 2 of the paper's body. I have not numbered the title page, outline page, or works cited page.

- [ ] I have read my outline, checking for parallel structure, punctuation, alignment, and capitalization.

- [ ] I have checked each page of my research paper for misspelled words and incorrect punctuation.

- [ ] I have checked the margins on each page to be sure that they are in accordance with my teacher's instructions.

- [ ] I have looked at my paper carefully and made changes to improve word choice.

- [ ] I have checked my paper for errors in sentence structure as well as parallel structure.

- [ ] I have checked to make sure that my parenthetical documentation is written and punctuated correctly.

- [ ] I have checked for accuracy in my direct quotations and paraphrased material.

- [ ] I have checked for organization and transition in my paragraph development.

- [ ] I have checked my works cited page to make sure that all the sources I used are listed. I have also made sure that the sources are correctly written, punctuated, and alphabetized.

Take Time to Evaluate

Read your paper one more time. This time, use a rubric or checklist to make sure you have met all the requirements for the assignment.

15 Polish your paper.

16 Evaluate your work.

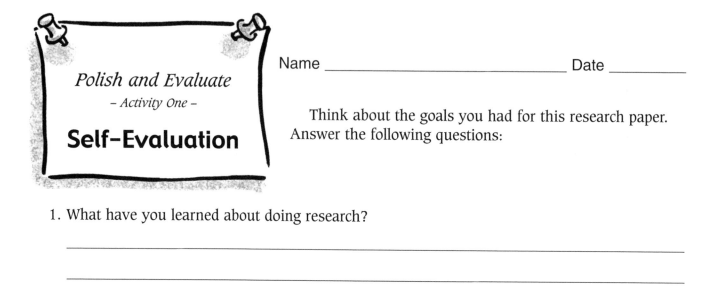

Name _____ Date _____

Polish and Evaluate
– Activity One –

Self-Evaluation

Think about the goals you had for this research paper. Answer the following questions:

1. What have you learned about doing research?

   _____

   _____

2. What changes will you make for the next research paper? Why?

   _____

   _____

3. What is the best part of your research paper? Why?

   _____

   _____

4. How have your research skills changed?

   _____

   _____

5. What additional topics or parts of your research would you like to know more about? Why?

   _____

   _____

6. What was most difficult in researching this paper? Why? How was the difficulty overcome?

   _____

   _____

   _____

7. What was the most difficult part of writing your paper? Why? How was the difficulty overcome?

   _____

   _____

   _____

Name _____ Date _____

Work with a classmate to evaluate each other's final research paper. Check for errors in grammar, spelling, documentation, word choice, punctuation, and capitalization. Answer the following questions as you evaluate each other's paper.

A Cooperative Learning Activity

1. Does the research paper have a neat and clean appearance? If not, what improvements do you suggest?

   _____

   _____

2. Do you think the title is appropriate? Why or why not?

   _____

   _____

3. What is one thing you learned from reading your partner's research paper?

   _____

   _____

4. Do you think your partner addressed the thesis with enough detail and supporting information?

   _____

   _____

5. Are there any suggestions you can make to improve your partner's paper?

   _____

   _____

6. Does the concluding paragraph restate the thesis sentence? If not, what do you recommend?

   _____

   _____

7. After reading your comments about your partner's paper, will these comments help you in evaluating your own research paper?

   _____

   _____

How to Write a Great Research Paper, Revised Edition

Presenting Your Research

Oral Presentation

After you have finished writing your research paper, you may be asked to deliver an oral presentation of your findings. Follow these basic steps as you prepare your presentation.

1. State the research paper topic.

2. Tell why you chose this topic.

3. State the thesis statement or general purpose of the research paper.

4. Give a brief account of the entire paper.

5. What conclusion(s) did you reach after completing this research?

6. Has this research encouraged or sparked an interest to continue further investigation of your topic?

7. Do not read your paper as your presentation; instead, rely on prepared notes.

8. Keep your audience in mind by using eye contact throughout your presentation.

9. Answer any questions that your classmates may have if your teacher allows the time.

10. Recognize any key sources that were helpful in writing your paper.

11. Stay within your time limit (usually two to five minutes); practice with a recorder or with a friend.

12. Use audio-visuals (posters, pictures, videos, charts, graphs, recordings) to enhance your presentation.

13. Describe the most interesting part of your research paper.

14. Make suggestions that you might offer to a classmate who is about to begin work on a research paper for the first time.

17 **Present your research.**

Using Note Cards in a Presentation

The audience wants to listen to an interesting speaker. Therefore, do not just stand up and read your paper aloud! Reading your paper aloud is likely to bore your audience. They might as well just read it themselves!

Instead, use note cards to organize your presentation and summarize the information from your research paper.

1. On the note cards, list the major points in your paper.
2. Do not write complete sentences on the note cards. Instead, write only a few words that will prompt you when speaking.
3. Using a dark pen or pencil, write large letters so that you can see the words easily.
4. As you finish with a note card, place the card on the bottom of the stack or turn the card over and create a second pile.

Overcoming Your Fear of Public Speaking

Being prepared is the best way to overcome nervousness or fear of public speaking. Take the time to practice in front of a mirror, with family members, before one or two friends, or even in front of your pet. Ask others to give you suggestions for ways to improve your presentation. Incorporate their suggestions into your next practice session.

Another helpful practice method is to record your practice session and play it back so that you can critique yourself.

Be sure to speak clearly, loudly, and slowly.

The more you practice, the more comfortable you will become with your speech.

Computer Presentations

A computer slideshow is one way to present your research, and it can also make a wonderful addition to an oral presentation. Microsoft® Power Point and Corel® Presentations are two programs commonly used for electronic presentations. Graphics, sound, and video can be added to the slides.

As you plan your slideshow, consider using the following:

- Informative graphics, such as charts, graphs, or tables dealing with your topic.

- Illustrations, such as drawings or photos, to visually support your topic.

- Simple, uncluttered screens. Do not fill your computer presentation with large amounts of text that might distract from what you are saying in your oral presentation.

In order to store or transfer an electronic presentation, you should be aware of the methods below. Be sure to follow your teacher's instructions.

- E-mail (A saved presentation can be attached to an e-mail message.)

- Website (You can create a website that enables your audience to view the presentation on the Internet.)

- Flash drive (A flash drive can hold large amounts of information.)

How to Write a Great Research Paper, Revised Edition

Index

= student activity page

Resources for Teachers

Here are some time-saving, teacher-tested resources that will facilitate successful student research. Be sure to keep parents informed, and share the evaluation tools you will use with the students BEFORE they begin their research.

Sample Parent Letter — page 106

Reproduce the sample letter and send it home to parents before assigning the research paper. It is important that parents understand the processes you are teaching to students. Communication before an assignment eliminates misunderstandings about your expectations.

Evaluation Rubrics — pages 107–109

Use the checklists and rubrics as models for evaluating student research papers. It is helpful to develop rubrics with your students before they begin writing their papers. That way, they understand how they will be evaluated up-front. Also, students may evaluate their own papers independently and then compare and discuss their evaluations with yours.

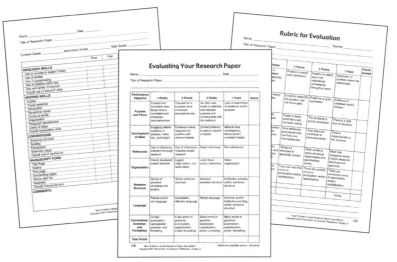

Answer Key — pages 110 and 111

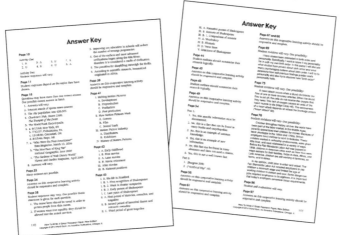

Dear Parents,

Soon your child will begin working on a research paper in my class. Fear not! We will get through this process together. Despite its challenges, this process is going to be an exciting and rewarding experience for your child.

The research paper is a step-by-step process through which I will carefully guide your child. However, I would like for you also to be involved and become an integral part in this writing process. You can help by making sure your child visits the library and uses reliable online resources, and by questioning and sharing the collected information at home. The research skills your child is about to learn will prove useful throughout his or her life—far beyond the walls of our classroom.

Some of the materials that we will need while completing the research process include the following:

- dictionary
- thesaurus
- index cards or strips of paper
- pens and pencils
- lined and plain paper
- computer, or access to a computer
- file folder

Once we begin the research project, please check periodically with your child to see how he or she is doing. If I can provide additional assistance in any way, please do not hesitate to call me at school.

Thank you for your support and encouragement.

Respectfully,

Name _____ Date _____

Title of Research Paper _____

_____

Content Grade: _____ Mechanics Grade: _____ Total Grade: _____

	Poor	Fair	Good	Excellent
RESEARCH SKILLS				
Use of sources to support thesis				
Use of quotes				
Use of paraphrasing				
Use of citations within text				
Use and variety of sources				
Overall use of research skills				
WRITING SKILLS				
Outline				
Thesis sentence				
Introduction				
Transitional words				
Choice of words				
Organization				
Paragraph development				
Clarity of ideas				
Overall writing composition skills				
CONVENTIONS				
Sentence structure				
Spelling				
Punctuation				
Grammar usage				
Overall use of mechanics				
MANUSCRIPT FORM				
Title Page				
Outline				
First page				
Succeeding pages				
Works cited list				
Neatness				
Overall manuscript form				

COMMENTS:

Evaluating Your Research Paper

Name _____ Date _____

Title of Research Paper: _____

_____

Performance Objective	4 Points	3 Points	2 Points	1 Point	Score
Purpose and Focus	Creates and maintains clear focus; tone is consistent and enhances persuasiveness	Focused on a purpose; tone enhances persuasiveness	An effort was made to establish and maintain purpose and communicate with the audience	Lack of awareness of audience and/or purpose	
Development of Ideas	Engaging details; evidence of analysis, reflection, and insight	Evidence clearly supports the position with relevant details	Limited evidence is used in support of details	Minimal idea development, limited and/or unrelated details	
References	Use of references indicates thorough research	Use of references indicates ample research	Some references	Few references	
Organization	Clearly developed overall structure	Logical organization, but lacks clarity	Lacks focus and/or coherence	Weak organization	
Sentence Structure	Variety of sentence structures and lengths	Varied sentence structure	Awkward sentence structure	Ineffective wording and/or sentence structure	
Language	Precise and/or rich language	Acceptable, effective language	Simple language	Incorrect and/or ineffective wording and/or sentence structure	
Conventions, Grammar, and Formatting	Correct punctuation, capitalization, grammar, and formatting	A few errors in grammar, punctuation, capitalization and/or formatting	Some errors in grammar, punctuation, capitalization, and/or formatting	Many errors in grammar, punctuation, capitalization, and/or formatting	
Total Points					

How to Write a Great Research Paper, Revised Edition

Maximum possible score = 28 points

Rubric for Evaluation

Name _____ Teacher _____

Title of Research Paper: _____

_____

	4 Points	3 Points	2 Points	1 Point	Points Earned
Position Statement	Position is clearly stated and consistently maintained.	Position is stated and maintained.	Position is stated, but is not maintained consistently throughout work.	Statement of position cannot be determined.	
Supporting Information	Evidence clearly supports the position.	Evidence supports the position, but not thoroughly.	Evidence is given, but limited.	Evidence is unrelated and/or unclear.	
Organization	Paper is well organized and developed.	Paper is developed fairly well, but lacks clarity.	The structure is poorly developed.	There is a total lack of structure.	
Tone	Tone is consistent and enhances persuasiveness.	Tone enhances persuasiveness, but there are inconsistencies.	Tone does not contribute to persuasiveness.	Tone is inappropriate to the purpose.	
Sentence Structure	Sentence structure is correct, and a variety of structures are used.	Sentence structure is generally correct.	Work contains some structural weaknesses and grammatical errors.	Work has numerous errors in both sentence structure and grammar.	
Punctuation and Capitalization	Punctuation and capitalization are correct.	There are very few errors in punctuation and/or capitalization.	There are several errors in punctuation and/or capitalization.	There are numerous errors in punctuation and/or capitalization.	
				TOTAL	

Teacher Comments: _____

_____

_____

Answer Key

Page 10

Activity One

1. A	3. A	5. U	7. A
2. U	4. U	6. U	8. A

Activity Two
Student responses will vary.

Page 11
Student responses depend on the topics they have chosen.

Page 18
Questions may have more than one correct answer. One possible correct answer is listed.

1. Answers will vary.
2. Internet search of sports news sources
3. The city population was 420,003.
4. *Charlotte's Web, Stuart Little, The Trumpet of the Swan*
5. World Book Encyclopedia
6. a. 9/17/68; New York, NY
   b. 7/12/37; Philadelphia, PA
   c. 12/18/46; Cincinnati, OH
   d. 8/19/46; Hope, AR
7. a. "Who Were the First Americans?"
      Time Magazine, March 13, 2006
   b. "The New Face of King Tut"
      National Geographic, June 2005
   c. "The Gardens of Walt Disney World"
      Flower and Garden Magazine, April 2005
8. Answers will vary.

Page 23
Many answers are possible.

Page 34
Answers on this cooperative learning activity should be responsive and complete.

Page 38
Student responses may vary. One possible thesis statement is given for each question.

1. The ozone layer should be saved in order to protect people from skin cancer.
2. If women want true equality, they should be allowed into the armed services.
3. Improving sex education in schools will reduce the number of teenage pregnancies.
4. One of the earliest and most advanced civilizations began along the Nile River; therefore it is considered a cradle of civilization.
5. The penalties for shoplifting outweigh the thrills.
6. According to scientific research, humankind originated in Africa.

Page 39
Answers on this cooperative learning activity should be responsive and complete.

Page 41
I. Making Motion Pictures
   A. Development
   B. Pre-production
   C. Production
   D. Post-production
II. How Motion Pictures Work
   A. Camera
   B. Film
   C. Sound Track
III. Motion Picture Industry
   A. Distribution
   B. Exhibition
IV. History of Motion Pictures

Page 42
I. A. Early childhood
I. B. First movies
II. A. Later movies
II. B. Movie retirement
III. A. After Movies
III. B. National positions

Page 43
I. A. His life in Stratford
I. B. 1. First recognition of Shakespeare
I. B. 2. Work in theater companies
I. B. 3. Early poems of Shakespeare
I. C. Last years of Shakespeare
II. A. First period of histories, comedies, and tragedies
II. B. Second period of historical drama and romantic comedies
II. C. Third period of great tragedies

Answer Key

III. A. Narrative poems of Shakespeare
III. B. Sonnets of Shakespeare
III. B. 1. Composition of sonnets
IV. A. Vocabulary
IV. B. Rhetoric
IV. D. Verse form
V. Criticisms of Shakespeare

Page 44

Student outlines should summarize their research logically.

Page 45

Answers on this cooperative learning activity should be responsive and complete.

Page 48

Student outlines should summarize their research logically.

Page 49

Answers on this cooperative learning activity should be responsive and complete.

Page 54

Part 1:

1. Yes, this specific information must be documented.
2. No, this is a fact that can be found in many books and encyclopedias.
3. No, this is an example of common knowledge.
4. Yes, this is an example of new information.
5. No, this fact can be found in many almanacs and does not need a citation.
6. Yes, this is not a well-known fact.

Part 2:

1. (Burgess 208)
2. ("Artificial Hip" 10)

Page 56

Answers on this cooperative learning activity should be responsive and complete.

Page 61

Answers on this cooperative learning activity should be responsive and complete.

Page 67 and 68

Answers on this cooperative learning activity should be responsive and complete.

Page 69

Student revisions will vary. One possibility:

I have always been interested in birth order and personality. Specifically, I want to know if my personality fits in with my own birth order. In this paper I will discuss what studies have proven about birth order and what many psychologists believe about birth order. I will try to determine how well previous findings predict one's personality and also try to discover new "birth order" personality traits.

Page 75

Student revisions will vary. One possibility:

A heart attack occurs when a blood clot blocks the flow of one or more coronary arteries. When the blood flow is cut off, the cells do not receive the oxygen that they need. This lack of oxygen causes an area of the heart muscle to die (Mayo Clinic 45). The seriousness of a heart attack depends on where the blockage occurs ("Heart Attack" 62).

Page 76

Student revisions will vary. One possibility:

Children throughout history all over the world have been part of the labor market. In the Middle Ages, parents apprenticed their children for money. Because of labor shortages in the 1600s and 1700s, British employers hired children to work in factories. These children worked in unhealthy environments, were given little food, and were mistreated in a variety of ways. Before the Fair Standards Labor Act was passed in 1938, children in American cities such as New York were wage earners for their families. Today in Asia, Africa, and Latin America, children are still working in factories, on farms, and in mines.

In my opinion, child labor is unfair and unjust. The Fair Standards Labor Act required employers to pay children a minimum wage and limited the age of working children to sixteen and over. Some dangerous jobs required employees to be eighteen. It is important that today's employers remember those requirements.

Page 96

Student self-evaluations will vary.

Page 97

Answers on this cooperative learning activity should be responsive and complete.

Common Core Connections

Grades 6-12 English Language Arts Common Core State Standards
Supported by the Information and Processes in this Book

Anchor Standard	Standard	Corresponding Grade 7 Standards
CCRA.R.1-3	Reading: Key Ideas and Details	RL.6-12.1-3; R.I.6-12.1-3
CCRA.R.7-9	Reading: Integration of Knowledge and Ideas	RL.6-12.7-9; RI.6-12.7-9
CCRA.R.10	Reading: Text Complexity	RL.6-12.10; RI.6-12.10
CCRA.W.1-2	Writing: Text Types and Purposes	W.6-12.1-2
CCRA.W.4-6	Writing: Production and Distribution of Writing	W.6-12.4-6
CCRA.W.7-9	Writing: Research to Build and Present Knowledge	W.6-12.7-9
CCRA.W.10	Writing: Range of Writing	W.6-12.10
CCRA.SL.1-3	Comprehension and Collaboration	SL.6-12.1-3
CCRA.L.1-2	Language: Conventions of Standard English	L.6-12.1-2
CCRA.L.3	Language: Knowledge of Language	L.6-12.3
CCRA.L.4-6	Language: Vocabulary Acquisition and Use	L.6-12.4-6